'A most helpful text for assistants who so often feel that they carry the responsibility for developing the skills and learning abilities of children with the greatest needs yet lack the training to do so effectively. Showing how to understand and consider the strengths and challenges of the 'whole' child, a documented pathway is set out. Educators and therapists can then see that which has been delivered, what has worked and what has not, then plan for further action where needed. I commend this work.'

– **Dr Lindsay Peer CBE**, C.Pyschol, C.Sci, AFBPsS, FRSA, FIARLD, AMBDA
Educational Psychologist

'This is a comprehensive, practical must have book for any teaching assistant working with children with SEND. It offers an in-depth overview of the role and responsibilities of additional support staff who are constantly developing new strategies and support pathways for our most vulnerable children.

This book will offer them all the support they need to understand the diverse needs of the children that they are working with in our 21st century classrooms and offer practical and simple techniques to meet their children's individual needs.

The book contains 8 chapters of very accessible text, charts, tables and diagrams. Each chapter will not only offer excellent professional development for a TA but also lots of practical activities to use with their children. Hopefully, it will empower support staff to feel confident to work much closer to teaching staff and be able to offer solutions that can become part of high quality teaching in every classroom.

An excellent resource for all members of support staff working with SEND children.'

– **Lorraine Petersen OBE**
Educational Consultant

'Full credit to the authors for highlighting such an important area of education. There is no doubt that every child deserves access to the most effective teaching and learning. Yet in SEND teaching there has been excellent research and provision for those children with the most severe learning difficulties but not always to every child with SEND. This book is unusual as it focusses on all children and their diverse needs and its aim is to raise attainment, give them equality and eventual independence. It is the result of the authors' own expert practice developed over 40 years in the classroom.

We have here a practical guide with accessible resources at the TA's fingertips. The structure is distilled into three light-hearted mnemonics ensuring quick reference. There is detail where needed but also the facility to dip in as may be practical. It is immediately useful, therefore, and long overdue.

Research in education carried out by practitioners is rare but much needed. Lack of time to research is so often the reason, somehow these authors have found the time. We all know teachers know best what their students need to progress. Here we have it. I can think of no better recommendation than that it comes from practitioners and for no more deserving group of youngsters. It is high time we had a core text for TAs who provide such vital support work for our children.'

– **Dr Elizabeth Sidwell CBE**, BSC(Hons), PGCE, FRSA, FRGS
Schools Commissioner for England (DFE 2011–13)

The Effective Teaching Assistant

Aimed at teaching assistants who work closely with children with special educational needs, *The Effective Teaching Assistant: A Practical Guide to Supporting Achievement for Pupils with SEND* is a practical and accessible resource tailored precisely for teaching assistants' specific needs, which explores both the opportunities and limitations presented by their role.

Each chapter provides both training activities and teaching resources designed to assist TAs/HLTAs in reflecting on their own experience while enhancing current practice. The chapters address key topics including

- SEND and inclusive teaching
- Multi-sensory teaching
- Supporting differentiation and adaptive teaching.

Supplemented with checklists and useful diagrams, this text is essential reading for teaching assistants, students and practitioners. It is particularly relevant for students working in undergraduate, post graduate and professional development programmes.

Abigail Gray has spent over 20 years as a teacher and school leader. She now works as an author, independent SEND consultant and SEND Expert tutor for Best Practice Network's NASENCO Award. She speaks and writes on all issues related to SEND and inclusion. Her first book, *Effective Differentiation*, was published in 2018.

Melanie Wright is a practising SENCO of 15 years. She has worked across six schools in both the State and Independent sectors, from Nursery through to Sixth Form and has been part of the Senior Leadership Team for eight years. She is also a Level 7 Exams Access Arrangements assessor for GCSEs and A Levels, and completed her NASENCO and Masters in Special and Inclusive Education at the Institute of Education.

The Effective Teaching Assistant

A Practical Guide to Supporting Achievement for Pupils with SEND

Abigail Gray and Melanie Wright

LONDON AND NEW YORK

First published 2021
by Routledge
2 Park Square, Milton Park, Abingdon, Oxon, OX14 4RN

and by Routledge
52 Vanderbilt Avenue, New York, NY 10017

Routledge is an imprint of the Taylor & Francis Group, an informa business

© 2021 Abigail Gray and Melanie Wright

The right of Abigail Gray and Melanie Wright to be identified as authors of this work has been asserted by them in accordance with sections 77 and 78 of the Copyright, Designs and Patents Act 1988.

All rights reserved. No part of this book may be reprinted or reproduced or utilised in any form or by any electronic, mechanical, or other means, now known or hereafter invented, including photocopying and recording, or in any information storage or retrieval system, without permission in writing from the publishers.

Trademark notice: Product or corporate names may be trademarks or registered trademarks, and are used only for identification and explanation without intent to infringe.

British Library Cataloguing-in-Publication Data
A catalogue record for this book is available from the British Library

Library of Congress Cataloging-in-Publication Data
A catalog record for this book has been requested

ISBN: 978-0-367-48844-4 (hbk)
ISBN: 978-0-367-48846-8 (pbk)
ISBN: 978-1-003-04314-0 (ebk)

Typeset in Sabon
by Apex CoVantage, LLC

Visit the eResources: www.routledge.com/9780367488468

For our children
Rebekah, Nathan and Mim

Contents

Checklists and audits

Acknowledgements

We would like to offer sincere thanks to our families for their patience and support during this long process. We are back in the room!

Illustrations

We are delighted to have original illustrations by the hugely talented Bug Shepherd-Barron. We are so grateful to Bug for their patience and creativity and thrilled to be able to share these wonderful, thought provoking images.

How to use this book

We are very much aware of the fact that time is short in school. Every minute counts. It may be that you have very little time to read, to plan or even to think when you are in the activities of the day to day classroom.

Audience

Teaching assistants (TAs) go by many different names. This book is aimed at everyone who is employed to support learners with SEND in the classroom; Learning Support Assistants (LSAs), Learning Assistants (LAs), Learning Support Workers (LSWs), Learning Mentors (LMs), Higher-Level Teaching Assistants (HLTAs) and Special Support Assistants (SSAs). We use the term TA as a shorthand throughout the book.

Editable online resources

Instead of the traditional photocopied resources or online PDF templates, the prompt sheets and checklists we have created are saved in a format that you can edit, save and print. The URL you need is in the front of the book on the copyright page. There are versions of them for reference in the run of text, but we have included blanks too, in case you prefer to write longhand.

Chapter summaries

Each chapter ends with a brief, bullet-pointed summary. We hope that if you need to miss a section, you might read the summary and then refer back to the key elements, resources or information, as we have signposted the materials we think are most important.

Helpful information boxes

There are glossary boxes in some chapters. In this way we explain technical terms and any jargon as we go along. It always seems like a good idea to have a glossary at the back, but we felt this was more immediate and usable.

Introduction

When Melanie and I embarked upon this project we could never have imagined that we were going to find ourselves completing the work remotely, via Facetime, in lockdown. In writing this book about supporting learning, I have come to understand (especially over the last few weeks) that effective support is a genuine collaboration. The thing I least enjoyed whilst working on my last book was the solitary nature of the task; weeks spent alone at my desk, reading, drafting and redrafting. One of the lessons to be learned from the lockdown experience of working at home and social distancing has to be about the value of shared experiences and how much we have to gain from working together. The huge value, reassurance and creativity that comes from the seemingly incidental back and forth between colleagues or friends, from the shared personal and individual perspectives, are the powerful opportunities for learning to be found even in conflict. Of course, the success of collaboration is defined by a number of characteristics: respect, listening, reliability, honesty, humour and of course, a shared goal. I am blessed with a professional partner who delivers every time, in every respect.

In common with almost every other parent in the nation I am suddenly in the position of watching my (adult) child participate in online learning. The trials and tribulations of attempting to fulfil the requirements of a degree in design without a studio, materials or real-time teaching are many. However, the thing that poses the biggest problem for this generation of displaced undergraduates would appear to be that they are having less opportunities to share their thoughts and create solutions together. I can see all too clearly the deep frustration, and actually the sadness, at this loss, each day, on my daughter's face. It has had the effect of further convincing me that while academic learning is a substantial part of school, working with peers and forming working relationships with peers is at least as important.

The message of this book speaks exactly to that. Pupils with SEND have a right to be included in a mainstream setting. That inclusiveness has to have, at its core, the genuine opportunity to negotiate that mainstream setting with the independence necessary to make connections with peers. It might seem like this focus on independence might threaten the TA role, but this couldn't be farther from the truth. We know that independence in learning can be a battle for pupils with SEND. They need the full support of everyone to achieve this aim. In these pages we have attempted to set out a structured approach to a TA's in-class support role, which respects and acknowledges the depth and complexity of special educational needs, but makes room for the expression of vulnerability which lies at the heart of independent learning.

Melanie and I come to this work from different professional backgrounds but with a wealth of shared perspectives about SEND. Both English teachers, we quickly moved to specialise in working with children with learning difficulties.

After completing a secondary PGCE in English 25 years ago, she took up her first teaching post in a mixed comprehensive in London, and quickly became interested in pupils with SEND. She became fascinated by her pupils and their diverse range of needs and was drawn to the challenge of understanding their specific difficulties, cognition and potential. We feel strongly that while the academic, social and cultural demands of school are difficult enough for most children, for those with SEND this is intensified. Making their path through education more accessible, and more successful, is the principle we share and that has sustained Melanie throughout 20 years as a SENCO, across six different schools, both State and Independent. She has taught in every phase, from Nursery to 18. Whilst working she has continued to study and gain as much knowledge and experience as possible about SEND: completing the Level 5 OCR qualification in specific learning difficulties, followed by the Level 7 exam access arrangement qualification, the National Award for Special Educational Needs Coordinators and recently a Masters in Special and Inclusive Education at IOE.

In the early 1990s, after graduating I started volunteering at a local school, reading with children with delayed skills. After two terms I joined the staff as a TA and worked under the close supervision of a fantastically energetic and committed SENCO. She harnessed every resource at her disposal to address the needs of a tide of children who had managed to get to Year 7 without acquiring the reading skills they needed to access the secondary curriculum. More than 30% of that year's intake were at least four years delayed in their reading skills. That early experience literally woke me up to the advantage that I had experienced as a child; acquiring literacy quickly, supported by parents who were devoted to my education. To meet so many children locked out of that experience and the opportunities it affords was a shock; it didn't even feel like a career decision, it was obvious, I had to become a teacher. This journey began for me the following year when I started working as a teaching assistant and has taken me though each layer of management to Headship and now consultancy.

Like me, often teaching assistants don't plan to become so while at school or college; it seems to be a vocation that we discover along the way. The many, many teaching assistants I have known and worked with, those I've met in training and those I meet at events, seem to share this strong sense of vocation. This personal commitment resonates with me and I think it is sometimes overlooked and often undervalued.

Making sure that teaching assistants occupy a space in which they are valued, championed, challenged and developed is hard work for SENCOs. TAs are not paid on the same scale as teachers and often have very limited opportunities for progression. Clearly, the advantages to having an effective team of TAs are obvious; their levels of commitment and motivation can translate into a workforce that offers support to the school and its pupils beyond the remit of any job description. As a SENCO, a Deputy and a Head, I benefitted from teams of TAs who approached their duties with compassion and commitment. This was apparent in so many ways; offers of assistance after school, attending pupil performances, moving furniture, caring for pupil or colleagues when they were upset or unwell, visiting children or parents at home and engaging in the wider community to raise funds. This kind of involvement requires respect and acknowledgement.

As we know from research and from experience, SENCOs and teachers greatly value their support staff. Following concerns raised by educational researchers about the limited impact of TA support on pupil attainment, teachers were the first to voice their support for maintaining TA numbers.

It would appear that TAs have an interesting duality of duty, both in supporting teachers and offering academic and pastoral support to vulnerable pupils. Perhaps something research had failed to quantify is the broader impact of TAs on the workplace, morale or, indeed, the workload of teachers.

Unfortunately, despite their popularity with teachers and indeed with pupils, TAs can find themselves in an unenviable position where the expectations of their employers and the measures of their success are not quite clear. It is possible for TAs to be placed at the centre of a provision for pupils with SEND without the training and support they need to deliver success. Difficulties arise sometimes from too great a variety of responsibilities, a lack of clarity in terms of authority and under-representation in management structures.

TAs often find it difficult to grasp and to quantify their own value, the substantial influence that they have on academic outcomes and children's development. This book aims to offer TAs a way to enhance their competence and to offer an accessible, professional language for them to use when going about their daily duties and talking to others about their experiences.

After a brief dip in numbers it would appear that a significant TA workforce is going to be a permanent feature of British schools for some time. 2020 appears to be the year we wake up to the realisation that the most highly paid members of our society are not necessarily those we most value. This has to be the year of the Key Worker, the year we acknowledge and celebrate the women and the men who dedicate their time and effort to their work not because of money, status or celebration but because it is the good and the right thing to do. TAs and indeed teachers across the country belong to this group. It's time we find a way to recognise the value of integrity and personal commitment to the betterment of others.

We hope that this work serves to empower TAs and help them to realise their importance, their potential and their value in supporting the most challenging and vulnerable children. It is in this spirit that we offer this book.

1 What do TAs need to know about special educational needs and disability?

SEND basics

While no TA, or indeed classroom teacher, is expected to become an expert in SEND, having some awareness of the way the system has evolved, and its basis in law, can be a genuine advantage. A clear understanding of the basics underpins good practice in all respects.

As a school-wide provision, rather than a subject-based department or phase, school arrangements for SEND are made in direct reference to educational law and the governmental guidance produced by the Department for Education (DFE).

The SEND Code of Practice refers to the commitment of the UK Government to the 'inclusive education of disabled children and young people and the progressive removal of barriers to learning and participation in mainstream education' (Education, SEND Code of Practice: 0-25 years, 2014, pp. 1.25,26) under Articles 7 and 24 of the United Nations Convention of the Rights of Persons with Disabilities.

The legal right to a mainstream education for children with SEND was established following the Warnock Report of 1978, and is included in the subsequent Education Acts of 1981 and 1993. The existing definitions relating to SEND formed part of the Education Act of 1996; this was superseded six years ago by the Children and Family Act (CAFA) 2014 (Government, 2014).

The CAFA 2014 sets out the explicit duties in respect of children with SEND. The duty on schools, along with those placed on Local Authorities (LAs) and other organisations, are described in the Special Educational Needs and Disability Code of Practice: 0–25 Years, 2020 (The Code) and this document relates directly to the CAFA.

The SEND Code of Practice: 0–25 Years (The Code) took effect on 1 September 2014, and details statutory guidance to organisations, including schools, relating to young people with SEND.

It relates to Part 3 of the Children and Families Act 2014 along with other regulations.

The Code refers to statutory duties placed on organisations regarding disabled children and young people by the Equality Act 2010.

What are the key terms?

It's very helpful to begin by getting an understanding of the key definitions contained in the CAFA. The definitions of a **special educational need,** a **learning difficulty** and **special educational provision,** along with a definition of **disability** are as follows:

Definition of Special Educational Needs (SEN)

Section 20 (1) of CAFA

A child or young person has SEN if they have a learning difficulty or disability which calls for special educational provision to be made for him or her.

Definition of a Learning Difficulty

Section 20 (2) of CAFA

A child of compulsory school age or a young person has a learning difficulty or disability if they:

(a) have a significantly greater difficulty in learning than *the majority of others of the same age*; or
(b) have a disability which prevents or hinders them from making use of educational facilities *of a kind generally provided for others of the same age in mainstream schools or mainstream post-16 institutions.*

Special Education Provision

Section 21 of CAFA

educational or training provision that is additional to, or different from, that made generally for others of the same age in -

Definition of disability

Section 6 (1) of the Equality Act 2010

A person (P) has a disability for the purposes of this Act if

- P has a physical or mental impairment, and
- the impairment has a substantial and long-term adverse effect on P's ability to carry out normal day-to-day activities (Section 6).

These terms are often conflated but it is important to see the distinctions; whilst they are related, they are NOT interchangeable.

A learning difficulty *may* or *may not* constitute a disability and, in either case, may or may not result in SEND and the implementation of a special educational provision (SEP).

In respect to schools, The Code refers to eight sections of the law, including the Equality Act 2010 (Government, Equality Act 2010) and the Special Educational Needs and Disability Regulations 2014 (Government, The Special Educational Needs and Disability Regulations 2014), as the relevant primary legislation. The Code explains *statutory* responsibilities placed upon schools[1] in terms of duties they 'must' perform.

As well as being required to identify and address the SEND of the pupils that they support, their 'must' duties include:

- use their best endeavours to make sure that a child with SEND gets the support they need – this means doing everything they can to meet children and young people's SEND
- ensure that children and young people with SEND engage in the activities of the school alongside pupils who do not have SEND
- designate a teacher to be responsible for co-ordinating SEN provision – the SEN co-ordinator, or SENCO (this does not apply to 16 to 19 academies)
- inform parents when they are making special educational provision for a child
- prepare an SEND information report and their arrangements for the admission of disabled children, the steps being taken to prevent disabled children from being treated less favourably than others, the facilities provided to enable access to the school for disabled children and their accessibility plan showing how they plan to improve access progressively over time (Education, SEND Code of Practice: 0-25 years, 2014, p. 92).

The CAFA and the guidance to schools provided in The Code is designed to enable pupils with SEND (whether or not they are in receipt of an Education, Health and Care Plan (EHCP)) to access an appropriate education, to 'achieve their best' (Education, SEND Code of Practice: 0-25 Years, 2014, p. 92) and to make a successful transition to the next stage of their lives with confidence.

What is an Education, Health and Care Plan?

When a school finds itself unable to make the appropriate provision for a child's SEND, an application can be made to the relevant LA to conduct an Education, Health and Care (EHC) needs assessment. If an EHC needs assessment takes place and results in an EHCP, the Plan *should* reflect a coordinated approach. This document should detail all aspects: educational, social and health care sectors. Also, it should fully describe a child's learning difficulties and the SEND that arises because of this difficulty or difficulties. The Plan should describe the child's:

- ✓ learning difficulties
- ✓ special educational needs
- ✓ the setting and provision required
- ✓ the details of additional curricular or specialist therapeutic support
- ✓ details of any social or health care provision

Who can request an EHC needs assessment?

A **parent**, a **young person** or a **school** may request that their LA conduct an EHC needs assessment. The LA must respond to the request within a six-week period, either agreeing or refusing to carry out the assessment.

How many school pupils have an EHCP?

It's important to look at these statistics carefully, bearing in mind that EHCPs are in place for young people beyond compulsory school age, up to the age of 25. Statistics on SEND for young people aged 19–25 years old in England, published in May 2020 (Education Health and Care Plans: England, 2020) recorded that 390,109 children and young people were in receipt of an EHCP.

In the calendar year 2019, LAs received 82,300 initial requests for an EHC needs assessment. This represents a 14% rise from the previous year. If an initial application is successful and the assessment takes place, the needs process is highly likely to result in an EHCP; in 2019, 94% of needs assessments resulted in a Plan. However, the most recent statistics show that 23% (18,800) initial applications were refused.

Of the 57,300 assessments made, 94% or 53,900, resulted in a new Plan.

The process of an EHC needs assessment is far from perfect and can sorely test the resilience of schools and families. This is not simply a matter of opinion but recently an explicit finding of a parliamentary select committee on SEND. The committee found that there were serious failings embedded in the current system, 'staff in schools and local authorities do not know the law, give misleading information or unlawful advice, and in some cases, publish erroneous information on their website' (Special Educational Needs and Disabilities, 2020, pp. 3–4). The process is, or rather should be, tightly time limited but often can exceed the limitation set and may well result in conflict. In 2019 only 60.4% of Plans were issued within the 20-week time limit. As a result, a system designed to protect the rights of children and young people with SEND to a mainstream education too often becomes a serious bone of contention for children and families, schools and authorities, resulting in disagreements that require professional mediation or referral to the First-Tier Tribunal.

While it is unlikely that TAs would be asked to take independent responsibility for this process or even parts of it, understanding its relevance is important. This is mainly because if a TA is employed to support a specific child or number of children with EHCPs in place, it's likely that this TA time represents a hugely valued and a hard won special educational provision. This resource may form the core of the special educational provision made by the Plan, following months of negotiation with the LA.

Further, in cases like this and of those where children are going through an EHC needs assessment, there is likely to be TA involvement in the compilation of evidence presented. It seems unfair to ask TAs to participate in a process of evidence gathering if they are unclear about the purpose and audience.

If there is a dispute about either making an EHC needs assessment, or about a decision concerning an existing Plan, the parents or young person themselves may have a right to appeal against the decision to the SEND Tribunal (SENDIST). Only parents and young people hold this right of appeal; schools may not appeal decisions to SENDIST.

What is the SEND Tribunal (SENDIST)?

SENDIST is a chamber of the First-Tier Tribunal and forms part of the UK court system. LAs and families sometimes fail to come to agreement about SEND provision; that being the case, in specific circumstances young people and parents have the right to a formal appeal process following:

- a decision not to carry out an EHC needs assessment or re-assessment;
- a decision that it is not necessary to issue an EHCP following an assessment;

- the description of a child or young person's SEN specified in an EHCP;
- the special educational provision specified, the school or other institution or type of school or other institution (such as a mainstream school/college) specified in the plan or that no school or other institution is specified;
- an amendment to these elements of the EHCP;
- a decision not to amend an EHCP following a review or re-assessment;
- a decision to cease to maintain an EHCP.

It is unlikely that a TA would be asked to attend a tribunal; however, it is worth knowing that written feedback from staff and school reports are often included in the bundles of evidence submitted. The tribunal experience is a stark reminder of the vital importance of integrity, accuracy and clarity of written feedback. The panel can only make a decision based on the evidence submitted. Therefore, fair decisions can only be made in the light of reliable reporting on a child's characteristics as a learner, their attainment and progress, and the support they may already receive. Without wishing to dramatise, it is important to recognise that they are the potential audience for a teacher's or a TA's professional opinion, and the information they collect and record. This is true as soon as you step into the classroom to support pupils and make records about a pupil's behaviour, performance and learning.

What about pupils with SEND who *don't* have EHCPs?

TAs are deployed to work in school for a variety of reasons and in a number of different ways. Some work exclusively with one or a small number of children with identified SEND or EHCPs in place. Some work to support whole class groups, and some with those children whose needs are identified and being met within the school's offer; the children receiving 'SEND support'.

More than three times the number of school age children fall into the 'SEND support' category than have EHCPs. As of January 2019, Government statistics showed that 1,047,200 pupils were recorded on school registers of SEND as receiving SEND support. This was equal to 11.9% of the total pupil population (Special Educational Needs in England: January 2019, 2020). The SEND of these pupils, therefore, are expected to be met by the resources that exist within the school's existing budget – the school's existing SEND provision. It often falls to TAs to make some of the necessary adaptations and to provide support to meet their educational needs following a process of identification by teachers and SENCOs.

The categories of need as described in The Code are applied to this process of identification and SENCOs are asked to identify a primary need; one area of difficulty that is most evident, pressing and a clear priority for educators. Currently, the largest group of these children, representing 23%, have Speech and Language and Communication Needs (SLCN) as their primary need (Special Educational Needs in England: January 2019, 2020).

Whether or not schools are able to resource an appropriate and properly equipped provision for pupils at SEND support is difficult to measure. Pupil populations and profiles of need vary from year to year, meaning that there is an ongoing need for support and training with regards to SEND for all staff – including the all-important TA.

Categories of need

Category of Need	*Examples*
1. Cognition and learning	Moderate Learning Difficulty (MLD) Profound and Multiple Learning Difficulty (PMLD) Severe Learning Difficulty (SLD) Specific Learning Difficulty (SpLD) which includes: Dyscalculia, Dyspraxia, Dysgraphia, Dyslexia
2. Communication and interaction	Autism (ASD) Speech, Language and Communication Needs (SLCN) Specific Language Impairment (SLI)
3. Sensory and/or physical needs	Hearing Impairment (HI) Visual Impairment (VI) Multi-sensory Impairment (MSI) Physical Disability (PD) Medical Needs
4. Social, emotional and mental health (SEMH)	Adjustment Disorders (may have experienced or witnessed a stressful event or a big change in their life) Anxiety Disorders (may suffer from panic attacks, headaches or other physical symptoms as a result of stress) Obsessive-compulsive Disorder (OCD) ADHD or ADD (Attention Deficit Disorder) Opposition Defiance Disorder (ODD)

What is the history of 'inclusion'?

The term 'inclusion' is a relatively new one. The 1918 Education Act made schooling compulsory for the first time for all disabled children, and a number of special institutions were set up for these children outside of mainstream schools. However, by the second half of the 20th century, there was a major shift in attitude towards children with disabilities. The Warnock Report of 1978, and the subsequent 1981 Education Act, introduced the term 'special educational needs'. This promoted the idea that a child's educational needs should be considered and addressed in order to limit the impact of their disability or impairment. This led to more children with disabilities being educated in mainstream schools rather than in special institutions. What followed was an attempt at 'integration', whereby SEND pupils simply coexisted alongside non-SEND children. It is only fairly recently that integration has been challenged for failing to really incorporate and meet the educational needs of SEND pupils and 'inclusion' has been introduced to replace it. Ofsted defines an inclusive school as one in which 'the teaching and learning achievements, attitudes and well-being of every person matter' (Ofsted, 2000, p. 7). However, the reality of unifying and fully including those with SEND in the classroom with those who do not have a special need is an ongoing battle which is continually deliberated, challenged and questioned. Fundamentally, inclusive values of equality, compassion, wisdom, participation, respect and trust should be at the very heart of every school and underpinning all that happens in the classroom.

Notwithstanding the dominant ideology of inclusive education, recent research has identified a serious concern that pupils with SEND are still acutely vulnerable to all forms of exclusion; official and unofficial, permanent and temporary. Whilst there are statistics on disciplinary exclusions, with the exception of the grey area occupied by the practice of 'off-rolling', there are no statistics on how much time pupils with SEND spend outside the main classroom, away from the curriculum and away from their class teachers. Most schools have time-out spaces, corridors and support bases where children with SEND often find themselves. Models of inclusion have long included one-to-one and small group study that takes place while pupils without SEND are working with their class teacher. Perhaps the reality is that inclusive practice is a continuum rather than a fixed point.

What are the characteristics of inclusive teaching in mainstream schools?

When we talk about 'inclusion' or 'inclusive teaching' in relation to SEND, we refer to the inclusion of children and young people with SEND in *mainstream* education. Our education system purports to promote equality under the law and offer mainstream education as a right and an option for all (Florian, 1998). This is an important right for pupils with SEND and is to be valued and protected. However, in 2019, the figures revealed that just under half of pupils with an EHCP attend a mainstream school, as numbers attending state-funded special schools and independent special schools continues to rise. In the current educational climate, 'special' provision is increasingly becoming the parents' and child's preferred option. This says a great deal about the ability of the system to deliver on its aims.

What is 'inclusive teaching'?

The Code 2015 talks about the 'Graduated Approach' to be taken by teachers of pupils with SEND – this approach should be made up of processes that Assess, Plan, Do, Review (Education, SEND Code of Practice: 0-25 Years, 2014, p. 100). This cycle should mean that all reasonable measures are taken to ensure all pupils with SEND have access to High Quality Teaching (HQT) and success within the mainstream curriculum. A detailed explanation of the Graduated Approach and a TA's role in supporting it can be found in Chapter 6.

How much do you know about your school's provision for pupils with SEND?

It is quite possible that you are very familiar with the aims and processes in place in your school already. However, for those new to a school or new to the role, it is helpful to know about key documents that relate to the TA role as described in the advert or the job description. There may well have been a good induction that has already covered this, but we include the following checklist as a safety net. It's useful to be clear about where you can find the answers to some basic questions about how your school makes its SEND provision and fulfils its duties under The Code and the law. This allows you to see how your role, as a TA, fits into the broader context.

The first important step is to stop worrying about what you don't know or are unsure about; it's much better to ask a question than guess or act quickly on an assumption. Table 1.1 is called *Getting Started*. Working through it is a helpful way to develop your knowledge and understanding about SEND at your school. As you work through the checklist, you might like to date rather than tick the columns to record your continual professional progress.

Table 1.1 Getting Started

Questions	Yes	No	Information/Action
Have I read the school SEND policy and/or handbook?			
Have I read the school SEND Information report?			
Have I read the school's most recent inspection report?			

Questions	Yes	No	Information/Action
Have I read and understood my job specification?			
Have I met the school SENCO?			
Have I visited any onsite SEND facilities?			
Do I have a specific list of pupils to support?			
Am I clear about channels of communication with SEND staff?			

Note

1 Mainstream schools, maintained schools and academies that are not special schools, maintained nursery schools, 16 to 19 academies, alternative provision academies and Pupil Referral Units (PRUs).

Summary

What do TAs need to know about special educational needs and disability?

- Schools make provision for pupils with SEND according to a legal framework that refers to both international agreement and national law.
- When supporting pupils with SEND, the TA role can form part of this provision.
- The right to a mainstream education for children with SEND is enshrined in the Children and Families Act (CAFA) 2014.
- Schools have duties to uphold the law and have due regard to the guidance published by the Department for Education (page 6) – this guidance is in the form of the SEND Code of Practice. LAs also have duties under the law.
- 'Special educational needs', 'learning difficulties', 'special educational provision' and 'disability' all have legal definitions that are distinct and specific (page 5).
- Education, Health and Care Plans can be put in place to describe a pupil's SEND and to identify the setting. An EHCP must quantify and specify the special educational provision they require in the setting.
- Parents of children, young people and schools have the right to request that a LA makes an EHC needs assessment.
- In 2019, 3.1% of school pupils had an EHCP in place. This represents a rise from the consistent figure of 2.8% from 2007 to 2017 (Statements of SEN and EHC Plans: England, 2019, 2020).
- Some EHCPs identify support from a TA as the necessary special educational provision to meet a pupil's needs.
- When there is a dispute about an EHC needs assessment or a plan, parents of children and young people can appeal the LA's decisions to the SEND Tribunal.
- School records and reports are sometimes submitted to the tribunal as evidence.
- Children supported by TAs may not have EHCPs in place but may be on a register of children receiving 'SEND support'. Nationally, 11.9% of children are recorded as receiving SEND support (Special Educational Needs in England: January 2019, 2020).
- Inclusion and inclusive education should ensure that children with SEND are provided with access to High Quality Teaching and appropriate education that prepares them for the next stage in their lives.
- The 'Graduated Approach' described in The Code is designed to ensure that educators make provision for children with SEND, based on evidence, and that they plan and assess the impact of this provision in a continuous cycle.
- If part of your role as a TA is in supporting pupils with learning difficulties, understanding how your school organises its provision for pupils with SEND is an important first step, especially if you are providing in-class support or running interventions for these children.

Resources

Table 1.1 Getting Started

Questions	Yes	No	Information/Action
Have I read the school SEND policy and/or handbook?			
Have I read the school SEND Information report?			
Have I read the school's most recent inspection report?			
Have I read and understood my job specification?			
Have I met the school SENCO?			
Have I visited any onsite SEND facilities?			
Do I have a specific list of pupils to support?			
Am I clear about channels of communication with SEND staff?			

2 The professional TA

Why are TAs so important in making provision for pupils with SEND?

TAs form more than 25% of the total school workforce. In data published by the Department for Education (DFE) in June 2019 for the previous year, this total comprising teachers, support staff and TAs numbered 947,214 FTE (full time equivalent) posts; of those 263,913 were TAs. The number of FTE TA posts has grown every year since 2011. Primary school settings had 176,700 FTE TAs, with 45,900 in secondary schools and a further 39,400 in special schools (School Workforce in England: November 2018, 2020). It's important to remember that these numbers represent the resource in terms of FTE posts, as many TAs work part-time, and so it means that there are considerably more than 263,000 individuals involved in making this provision. TAs are part of a huge national team of colleagues and are certainly not alone in their efforts to manage this demanding role.

How has the TA role evolved?

In 2009, the Institute of Education and partners produced a report entitled 'The Deployment and Impact of Support Staff' (DISS) (Education I. o., 2009). It looked at the impact of all school-based support staff on pupil outcomes; this included TAs. It raised a number of concerns about the way TAs were deployed and trained across both primary and secondary settings. The report concluded that informal classroom support by TAs had a 'systematic' negative effect on progress in English, mathematics and science for pupils across all year groups and reduced teacher-to-pupil interaction (Education I. o., The Deployment and Impact of Support staff in Schools, 2009). There were a number of key issues identified; TAs were reactive rather than proactive, task-focused rather than aware of the bigger picture, and interactions with pupils were more likely to 'close down' rather than 'open up' learning conversations with pupils.

The Education Endowment Foundation published a report in 2015, 'Making Best Use of Teaching Assistants' (Sharples, Webster & Blatchford, 2015), that made seven recommendations about the most effective use of

TAs. These recommendations were subdivided into working in classrooms, one-to-one or small-group settings, and in making relevant connections between the two.

The guidance identified the need for more training and support for TAs so that they could work more effectively with pupils, encouraging them to develop strategies to work independently. Best practice for TAs was identified as supporting and supplementing teaching rather than taking on the teacher's role, particularly for those pupils with SEND.

Instead of deploying TAs to offer informal support for pupils with low attainment, schools were encouraged to use TAs to offer targeted support in small groups or one-to-one interventions (Sharples, Webster & Blatchford, 2015). Additionally, a key recommendation was that TAs should have access to training in the delivery-specific, evidence-based interventions, and take a role in helping pupils involved to make connections between the interventions and their independent classroom work.

TAs then, should:

- ✓ Enhance teaching not replace it
- ✓ Foster independence
- ✓ Enable teacher pupil relationship
- ✓ Help make links in learning
- ✓ Deliver evidence-based interventions.

Expectations placed upon teachers regarding pupils with SEND

To work successfully alongside teachers in supporting pupils with SEND, it's useful to understand the expectations placed upon them by their employers, the inspectorate and The Code.

September 2019 saw the introduction of a new Education Inspection Framework (EIF). This new framework contained some clear messages about SEND. Schools are expected to provide a curriculum which can be adapted and delivered in such a way that those pupils with SEND acquire both 'the knowledge and the cultural capital they need to succeed in life' (EIF, 2019, p. 9). Inspectors expect aspirations to be high for all pupils, including those identified as disadvantaged, and for school to prepare them 'for the next stage of education, employment or training' (EIF, 2019, p. 9).

In addition to Ofsted's requirements, there are also explicit professional Standards for Teachers. They divide into two sections; Standards for Teaching and Standards for Personal and Professional Conduct. Section 5 of the Teaching Standards is concerned with the specific responsibility to address the 'strengths and needs' of all students (Teachers' Standards, 2011, p. 11).

Expectations on teachers include to:

- ✓ differentiate appropriately;
- ✓ use effective approaches to teaching;

- ✓ know how to overcome a range of factors that inhibit learning;
- ✓ be aware of the physical, social and intellectual aspects of child development;
- ✓ recognise and adapt teaching to support pupils' education at different stages of development;
- ✓ have a clear understanding of the needs of all pupils (SEND, G&T, EAL) and be able to use and evaluate distinctive teaching approaches to engage and support them.

The Code also makes particular reference to the important role of all teachers in implementing the 'Graduated Approach' at all stages. All teachers should deliver 'high quality teaching targeted at . . . areas of weakness' (The Code, 2015, 6.18). *All* teachers are teachers of pupils with SEND.

Expectations placed upon TAs regarding pupils with SEND

Unlike teachers, TAs are not subject to an explicit set of regulatory standards. A set of standards was released by the Training and Development Agency for schools in 2010, outlining a range of *desirable* knowledge and skills for TAs. Following this, in 2014 the DFE set up a review of standards for TAs. Subsequently they chose not to publish them, preferring to allow Headteachers to decide how they should use and deploy TAs and to set their own standards for recruitment. Therefore, the criteria regarding the recruitment of TAs is as stipulated in The Education (Specified Work) (England) Regulations 2012, which define 'Specified work' within schools including those persons who plan, deliver and assess pupils and those working in support:

> (a) the person carries out such work in order to assist or support the work of a qualified teacher or a nominated teacher in the school (cite Regulation 3, Paragraph 6).

The standards for Higher-Level Teaching Assistants (HLTAs) had been introduced in 2003. These standards set out the same core themes as the draft standards for TAs from 2010. The Headteacher may have due regard to these HLTA standards when making a decision about the appropriateness of an appointment of either a TA or an HLTA.

When the Government decided against publishing revised standards in 2014, unions representing TAs issued their own draft standards focusing on the following thematic areas:

- ✓ Professional standards and conduct
- ✓ Knowledge and understanding
- ✓ Teaching and learning
- ✓ Working with others.

TAs are not subject to the same requirements as teachers in terms of qualifications, and while HLTAs (and sometimes even TAs) do undertake some whole class teaching, they are not paid according to the main pay spine. Further, TAs are often not required to attend all training, other than mandatory sessions on safeguarding, health and safety, etc., and are excluded from the teachers' pension scheme. They are able to join professional associations and unions. However, TAs do teach and support teaching, they inhabit the classroom and the staffroom and work directly with pupils, parents, external agencies and indeed with other staff.

Whilst there may be advantages in the lack of regulation, there is great value in knowing what is expected of the TA in their particular role. Without a clear idea about the demands of the job and the competencies required it is hard to be confident, to improve or to progress. We would always advise any employee to scrutinise their job description; it's often the case in schools that there are 'coverall' phrases that extend the duty of staff to a range of activities that are not explicit in the contract or offer of employment. TAs are often a case in point and schools frequently have to pull together. Schools are places where we have to be prepared for as many eventualities as possible but not everything is always foreseeable, no matter how great your risk assessments.

With all that in mind, Table 2.1 offers an opportunity to map the TA's experience or job specification against this framework. We have suggested that 'the standard' should be rated in terms of confidence and knowledge of each element, with a simple tick in the box to indicate competence and confidence and a (-) where there is room for improvement. In 'Comments', it's worth noting any

Table 2.1 TA Standards

	Rating	Comments
Personal and professional conduct		
Ethos policy practice		
Behaviours and attitudes		
Safeguarding		
Diversity		
Self-improvement (CPD)		
Knowledge and understanding		
Skills qualifications and experience		
Expertise in SEND – adaptation		
Knowledge up to date		
CPD		
Subject knowledge		
Role in classroom and whole school		
Teaching and learning – supporting		
Differentiation		
Extracurricular inclusion		

(*Continued*)

Table 2.1 (Continued)

	Rating	Comments
Behaviour management		
Assessment and planning		
Sensitive communication with pupils		
Contribute to teaching environment		
Working with others		
Recognise and respect roles of stakeholders		
Sharing information		
Informing planning and decision making		
Working with specialists		
Attendance reviews and TAC meetings		

action to be taken to address the gap. The gap might be closed by additional reading, collaboration with a member of staff or attending some online training. It might be closed by having a go at some of the activities in this book!

Belonging

Flexibility is at the heart of the TA role; it's at the heart of the majority of school-based roles. However, TAs often need to exhibit a very high level of flexibility and adaptability. It's usual for TAs to support pupils across more than one year-group, take an active part in more than one subject, and to offer support during unstructured time and in activities, playtime and trips.

Most teachers have a defined 'territory', whether it is the phase in which they specialise, their subject area or, indeed, their own teaching space. TAs learn to be 'at home' all over the school. The school makes an implicit rather than explicit expectation of TAs to understand how to function appropriately, everywhere from physical education to food tech, from assembly to phonics. In terms of routines, the location of equipment, health and safety expectations, this is a big ask. It's one of the features of the role that can offer huge advantages in terms of getting to know pupils. TAs can observe how *they* experience school and further, how they are different in different spaces and when facing different challenges.

'TAs learn to be 'at home' all over the school.'

If at all possible, new TAs need time to walk around the school, to go into the rooms in which they will be working, be offered induction into routines and offered the necessary advice about clothing, equipment and protocols for behaviour.

'Working with others' – the fourth standard

'Working with others' is central to the approach we suggest taking in the following chapters. In the standards it is exemplified by respecting the roles of stakeholders, information sharing, involvement in decision making, working with external agencies and specialists, and attending meetings. In this way it appears to focus on the importance of collaboration outside of the classroom within the structures that exist for planning and feedback. However, for TAs, working in the classroom *is* 'working with others'. To be effective, TAs must collaborate with teachers and pupils alike. It seems more practical to look at 'working with others' in the light of the TA's classroom role and how they might best contribute to and support differentiation in that setting.

'To be effective, TAs must collaborate with teachers and pupils alike.'

The practicalities of the working relationship between teacher, TA and pupil in the classroom are the focus of this work. Practical approaches to that end are discussed at length in the following chapters.

Summary

The professional TA

- It's important to understand the role of the TA and the teacher, specific to the setting.
- There are official standards for teachers and clear expectations regarding SEND set out by the DFE and by Ofsted.
- There are unofficial standards for TAs set out by voluntary organisations.
- The unofficial standards for TAs mirror the standards for HLTAs and are divided into four sections; Professional Standards and Conduct, Knowledge and Understanding, Teaching and Learning, and Working with Others.
- All TAs should have a job description; it is helpful to refer to this and consider it in the light of the unofficial standards.
- The role of the TA can vary enormously in different settings; however, being clear about their position and the expectations of the school is essential.
- Getting to know the environment is important for TAs as they often work school-wide and outside it; becoming familiar with a variety of spaces and protocols takes time.

Resources

Table 2.1 TA Standards

	Rating	Comments
Personal and professional conduct		
Ethos policy practice		
Behaviours and attitudes		
Safeguarding		
Diversity		
Self-improvement (CPD)		
Knowledge and understanding		
Skills qualifications and experience		
Expertise in SEND – adaptation		
Knowledge up to date		
CPD		
Subject knowledge		
Role in classroom and whole school		
Teaching and learning – supporting		
Differentiation		
Extracurricular inclusion		
Behaviour management		
Assessment and planning		
Sensitive communication with pupils		
Contribute to teaching environment		
Working with others		
Recognise and respect roles of stakeholders		
Sharing information		
Informing planning and decision making		
Working with specialists		
Attendance reviews and TAC meetings		

3 What do TAs need to know about core deficits?

It's no secret that pupils with SEND and specific learning difficulties (SpLDs) often underachieve; they fail to keep pace with their peers and have lower levels of attainment, experiencing fewer achievements at school (Special Educational Needs in England: January 2019). A key role for TAs working to support pupils with SEND is to assist in closing this gap.

SpLDs

Specific Learning Difficulties (SpLDs): a difficulty that occurs with a specific aspect of learning, such as numeracy, literacy, organisation, memory and time management. The most common SpLDs are:

Dyslexia – a specific pattern of cognitive difficulty that can affects phonology, memory and processing speeds (diagnosed by an educational psychologist or a specialist teacher with a relevant qualification).

Dyspraxia – otherwise known as **Developmental Co-ordination Disorder**, it affects a child's gross and/or fine motor skills and therefore their physical co-ordination. It can also affect their processing speeds and working memory (diagnosed by an occupational therapist).

ADHD/ADD – Attention Deficit Hyperactivity Disorder and Attention Definition Disorder are neurological conditions impacting a child's ability to focus and concentrate (diagnosed by a GP, a consultant paediatrician or a clinical psychologist).

Dyscalculia – characterised by difficulties in learning mathematical facts, numerical magnitude and concepts of number, counting, measuring, calculating and orientation (diagnosed by an educational psychologist).

Speech and Language Disorder – describes children with language difficulties which affect their communication and learning (diagnosed by a speech and language therapist (SALT) or a pathologist).

Autistic Spectrum Disorders – conditions that affect social interaction, communication, behaviour and interests (diagnosed by a consultant paediatrician or clinical psychologist).

First and most importantly, the term '**underachievement**' suggests that a pupil could achieve more and at a higher level. It hints at the significant difference that can exist between pupil ability and pupil attainment. Schools tend to measure and report to parents about pupil **attainment** – describing the level of knowledge and skills a pupil has demonstrated and can apply. In our experience, schools are much less likely to share data derived from measures of underlying ability or measures of Intelligence Quotient (IQ).

Underachievement: identification of pupil attainment lower than expected or predicted.

Attainment: a skill that has been learned or a goal achieved; this is often represented by a particular level or grade that is recognised within the class or judged against national norms.

In short, it's not always helpful, or indeed fair, to judge a pupil's capability by their current attainment, i.e. teacher assessments made against **age related expectations** (e.g. Below/Meeting/Exceeding). While measures of attainment may focus on literacy, numeracy and subject specific knowledge, measures of **underlying ability** focus on the speed and capacity of memory and **cognitive processing**. These underlying abilities can have a direct impact on the development of literacy, language and numeracy skills and are, therefore, relevant across the curriculum and can affect attainment across the full range of subjects.

Age related expectations: these expectations describe what an average child of a given age should have learned or be able to do.

Cognitive processing: this refers to the tasks that the brain does continually to process the information we receive from our environment.

Underlying ability: this refers to the various cognitive processes that underlie academic attainment; a student may have distinct strengths and weaknesses in relation to their cognition.

It's easy to think of poor reading, spelling, grammar, writing and numeracy as clear evidence of low intelligence or as markers of lower ability, but this is far from the truth. Individuals with high, even exceptionally high, levels of intelligence can struggle with all of those difficulties. This chapter explains why, and what to do about it in the classroom.

What has intelligence got to do with special educational needs?

The word intelligence comes from the Latin *intelligere* – to understand. Its definition is 'the ability to acquire and apply knowledge and skills' (Oxford English Dictionary, 2020). In this way, intelligence is distinct from attainment; intelligence is measured by 'the ability to acquire and apply'; attainment is a measure of what is known. It's a word well used in relation to education and in schools; however, it's not something that is easily described. In fact, the way we tend to think about intelligence and the measures we use in attempt to quantify it are subjects much debated by psychologists and neuroscientists. In that a core purpose of education is to develop the knowledge and skills of pupils, it's surprising that initial teacher training spends so little time considering it.

IQ is a score that defines intellectual ability and is a commonly used term, common enough for it to become the name of a TV quiz show. However, the origins of IQ and its initial purposes are much less well known. Initially developed in the late 19th and early 20th century, the process for modern IQ measurements and the widely used Wechsler Intelligence Scale for Children (WISC)[1] was first introduced in 1949. It comprises more than 10 different subtests, reflecting its author David Wechsler's belief that intelligence comprises a number of specific but interrelated functions.

Intelligence Quotient: IQ should provide a measure of reasoning skills 'in ways that minimise the advantage of prior knowledge'.[2] IQ tests comprise a number of measures.

In 2020, a full-scale IQ test is divided into five cognitive domains and takes an hour to complete. It is usually administered on a one-to-one basis by an educational psychologist (EP). The Weschler Intelligence Scale for Children which is now in its 5th edition primarily measures

- ✓ Verbal comprehension
- ✓ Visual spatial
- ✓ Fluid reasoning
- ✓ Working memory
- ✓ Processing speed

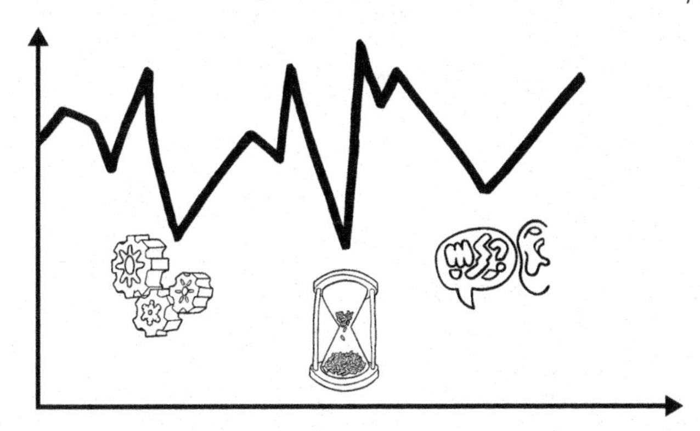

The EP will also consider, observe and comment on the child's history, behaviour, approach and attitude during testing.

It's very common for pupils who struggle with classroom learning to have low scores in respect to one or more of the areas outlined previously. Children with specific areas of significant weakness are sometimes described as having a 'spikey profile'. This means that instead of scoring at a similar level across the various subtests, they have high scores, average scores and low scores. When these are plotted on a graph, the line drawn shows peaks and troughs.

The lowest scores for children with specific learning difficulties are frequently in tests of:

- ✓ Working memory
- ✓ Phonological processing
- ✓ Processing time.

We refer to these key areas of '*core deficits*' due to the simple fact that they can be at the core of a great many barriers to learning. It's hard to think of a single barrier to cognition and learning not linked to one of these three: poor reading and spelling; lack of motivation; slow pace; lack of personal organisation; difficulties with time management; difficulties in following instructions – the list is seemingly endless.

Assessments for diagnosing difficulties

To those with little experience of the assessment process it can seem like its main purpose is to provide a child with a 'label' and assign them to a category of need. However, a full assessment of a child's attainment will usually include measures of:

- ✓ intelligence
- ✓ language function

- ✓ numeracy
- ✓ physical and or sensory abilities
- ✓ working memory.

The process is designed to identify any and all barriers to learning. Furthermore, it should offer some insight as to how these barriers might be overcome. A single diagnostic 'label' *may* be the result, but this can only ever be shorthand for the highly individual and specific set of information that is produced. Despite similarities in scores, patterns of scores, diagnoses and 'labels', no two children are exactly alike.

A detailed assessment should do three things:

- ✓ Identify the nature of the underlying abilities;
- ✓ Establish links between any areas of weakness and the causes for concern that lead to the referral;
- ✓ Outline practical strategies to assist the children and young people in overcoming the barriers to achievement.

Understanding the impact of core deficits on learning in the classroom

1. Working memory

Working memory is distinct from short-term memory in that it relates to the ability to actively work with 'in the moment' information, rather than simply remember it for a short time. It is sometimes referred to as executive functioning; the idea of receiving a piece of information, holding it in your head, whilst receiving other information or performing an action, and then delivering the outcome. It has been described as the brain's sticky note, a mechanism for capturing and parking necessary information.

Impact on learning

A pupil with *poor* working memory has a reduced capacity to store this temporary but important information. As a result, a child with poor working memory may struggle to plan and organise their schoolwork, their belongings or their time. Problems with working memory can affect a child's ability to cope with complex instructions, to prioritise, to analyse and to complete tasks, irrespective of flexible deadlines or extra time.

There has been much debate and research devoted to the question of whether or not it is possible to improve working memory capacity with therapeutic intervention and training. Irrespective of this ongoing research, there is evidence to show that there is a benefit in helping pupils to develop self-awareness and good strategies to support their working memory. TAs can help pupils to develop these good habits, to choose effective study skills and find individual strategies to make the most of the working memory capacity they have.

Impact on the learner

A poor working memory can be deeply frustrating for pupils. They may have the breadth and depth of knowledge to achieve but be regularly hindered by the demands placed on their working memory by school rules and conventions. The negative impact of constant reprimands due to forgotten and lost equipment, deadlines missed, slips not retuned, timetable changes, etc. can lead to disengagement with learning as a whole. The motivation and ability to focus on the knowledge and skills of the curriculum can be overshadowed by anxiety and frustration with issues of conformity. Deciding what is important and what needs to take up space in the working memory is key. Once the sticky note is full, it's full!

2. Phonological processing

From the Greek *'phono'* meaning *sound* or *voice*, phonological processing is the use of phonemes (units of sound) 'to **process** spoken and written language' (Wagner & Torgesen, 1987). Speech sound processing covers a range of sub-skills including awareness, which is the recognition of sounds; retention, the ability to remember them accurately; and retrieval, the process of finding and using the sounds accurately and translating them into letters or speech.

Impact on learning

It's pretty difficult to think of a mainstream classroom activity that doesn't in some way relate to the relationship between letters, sounds and meaning. Obviously, it's entirely possible to convey meaning with images and gesture alone; however, in a mainstream environment this mode of communication is most often used to meet specific sensory or language and communication needs, or to support spoken language. Classrooms tend to be full of printed, projected, painted, modelled and spoken words.

From the moment that they arrive in Nursery, children are immersed in a language rich environment. It's assumed that by the time children start in Reception that they have awareness of how to follow and interpret spoken language.

Further, there is also an assumption that language development grows and becomes more sophisticated with time spent at school. However, for those children with a specific phonological awareness problem, simply being immersed in language will not necessarily help them to improve and consolidate skills in the same way as other children.

These difficulties with awareness, retrieval and retention of speech sounds can be highly specific, and may come in any combination and alongside other difficulties.

This can often be confusing for teachers and TAs as pupils' language development may seem inconsistent as a result. There is a standard expectation for reading, spelling, writing and maths to progress at similar rates; however, children with phonological processing difficulties may exhibit inconsistency and do any, or all, of the following:

- ✓ read and write longer words (more than two syllables) *more easily* than two or three letter words (CVC words like c-a-t);
- ✓ rely upon whole word reading skills using the shape of a word to remember it while struggling to decode unfamiliar new words;
- ✓ mispronounce words but seem to understand and follow complex language;
- ✓ use age-appropriate language in speech but fail to use the same in written work;
- ✓ consistently misspell or vary the spelling of high frequency words.

Phoneme: the distinct unit of sound within a word. To decode an unfamiliar word, a pupil may break the word up into its individual phonemes before blending them together to make the word.

Orthographic reading and spelling: The ability to see the whole word and recognise it or reproduce it without the need to 'sound out' phonemes.

Given that TAs often work to support phonics programmes, it's important to recognise that there can be a great deal of discrepancy in what is heard, spoken, understood and written by a child with such difficulties. A child who manages to use, read and even write whole words may still struggle with phonemes out of context.

Impact on the learner

Clearly, poor phonological processing often leads to a delay in acquiring age-appropriate literacy skills. This often has a significant impact even beyond the more academic demands of school. There is often also an emotional or behavioural impact as the gaps in skills present themselves in the public environment of the classroom. As well as a degree of frustration and potentially confusion, children can experience a whole raft of emotions such as shame, embarrassment or a lack of self-esteem, which can lead to refusal to participate, fear of subjects or even school phobia leading to a drop in attendance or a rise in lateness. Sometimes avoidance is the go-to strategy either by delay or distraction, inside or outside the classroom.

3. Slow speed of processing

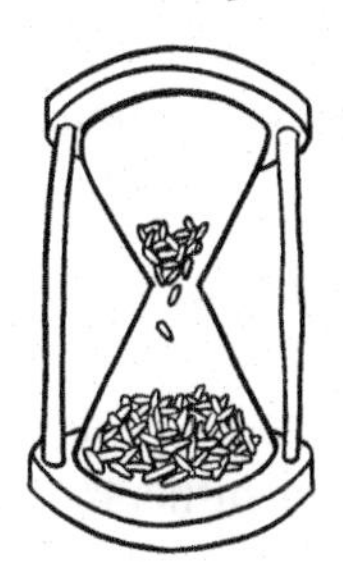

Children with slow speed of processing take longer to think about information and to respond to instructions and situations. It's important to note that slow speed of processing is just that; slow speed does not mean the *quality* or *accuracy* of processing is reduced. Just because a child or young person takes longer to respond does not mean that they are unable to understand or apply what is being taught. However, in the time pressured environment of the modern classroom, any delay can affect a pupil's performance and mask their ability.

Impact on learning

Clearly, slow pace of processing may be linked to the other core deficits. The labour-intensive nature of processing and organising a response can significantly slow even the most polished and accurate contribution. Pupils may be slow to answer or ask questions, to start work independently or manage group tasks to completion; often they do not finish work in the time given.

Impact on the learner

A child who is struggling to keep pace in terms of processing may seem disengaged as they struggle to participate in the classroom conversation, especially in whole class 'question and answer'. They may be characterised by a lack of consistency in their written responses, and the work in their books and projects may be patchy. Having omitted to do or to follow parts of processes, they may seem to lack understanding. This can manifest as a lack of motivation or, indeed, in anger or frustration as they fail to keep pace with the curriculum and their classmates.

Notes

1 Details of the WISC V can be found at the Pearson Clinical website: www.pearsonclinical.com/psychology/products/100000771/wechsler-intelligence-scale-for-childrensupsupfifth-edition-wisc-v.html
2 *What do IQ tests test?* Interview with Psychologist W. Joel Schneider by Scott Barry Kaufman. *The Scientific American: Beautiful Minds* 02/2014.

Summary

What do TAs need to know about core deficits?

- Children identified as having SEND often underachieve in comparison with their non-SEND peers. TAs often support pupils in attempting to close the gap in achievement.
- There are a number of underlying difficulties that may affect a pupil's ability to learn independently; to read, write and complete tasks at an age appropriate level.
- There is a difference between measures of academic attainment and measures of underlying ability.
- Learners with high levels of intelligence can struggle to develop age-appropriate numeracy and literacy in the presence of specific difficulties with memory and processing skills.
- Intelligence is described by the measurement of a person's verbal and performance skills; the tests investigate verbal comprehension, working memory, perceptual organisation and processing speed.
- Common areas of deficit that occur across a range of specific learning difficulties include poor working memory, poor phonological (speech sound) processing and slow processing times. We have referred to these three as 'core deficits'.
- Diagnostic assessments of a pupil's learning difficulties should identify the nature of the underlying difficulties, establish links between areas of weakness and causes of concern, and outline strategies to assist the pupil in overcoming these barriers to learning.
- Working memory relates to the pupil's ability to capture and retain information in order to use it to inform an action or response – it can be thought of as the brain's 'sticky note'.
- The impact of poor working memory is often a reduced capacity to store the vital information needed to plan and organise school work and belongings. This can lead to a great deal of frustration and underachievement.
- Phonological processing refers to a number of skills involved in the retention and retrieval of speech sounds.
- Poor phonological processing can impact spoken and written language as pupils struggle to establish the links between the sounds and letter shapes required for fluent reading and writing.
- This difficulty is often characterised by inconsistencies in spoken and written language.
- A pupil with slow speeds of processing will take longer to work through tasks irrespective of the quality or accuracy of their understanding.

4 How can TAs support multi-sensory teaching?

This chapter offers TAs an explanation of the theory of multi-sensory teaching and its impact on the progress and attainment of pupils with SEND.

The chapter identifies the need to consider the effect of the learning environment on pupils, encouraging sensory balance and avoiding overstimulation and distraction. TAs are invited to take part in a series of activities by which to evaluate and audit the sensory aspects of the classroom.

This chapter also includes a number of practical resources supporting this multi-sensory approach, which can be printed and used with pupils.

Why take a multi-sensory approach to teaching?

It's widely accepted that there are five basic human senses: sight, hearing, taste, touch and smell. These are ingrained in our general knowledge and feature in everything from children's books to TV and even in teachers' scaffolds for creative writing. We think about our senses as five distinct categories of input. This paradigm goes all the way back to Aristotle and seems to be impervious to change even in the light of scientific discovery. In reality, a contemporary understanding of our senses is more complicated in that it separates sensory reception and perception and adds new categories including balance, thermo-reception and pain. When a receptor cell receives a stimulus, this results in a sensation. Perception is processing this sensation into meaning.

A multi-sensory approach to learning refers predominantly to this philosophical concept of the five senses. We imagine the brain as a filing cabinet each file drawer is labeled with the name of a different sense: sight, sound, touch, taste and smell. Multi-sensory teaching deliberately connects knowledge to an experience via one or more of these senses. Knowledge connected to more than one sense is, therefore, stored in more than one drawer; the more drawers in which knowledge is filed, the more likely the knowledge it is to be retrieved by the owner of the filing cabinet.

At the beginning of the 20th century, Samuel Orton and Anna Gillingham developed the Orton-Gillingham method to teach initial reading skills (phonics) by explicitly linking letter sounds and shapes in a personalised and

multi-sensory process. This ensured that learning to read was not entirely dependent on looking and listening but that it was a tactile experience. This was thought to offer a bespoke learning experience by providing the learner with a variety of stimulus and the best possible chance of recall.

Examples of a multi-sensory approach might be:

- Creating letter shapes in sand;
- Making letters out of modelling clay;
- Holding coloured tissue in front of the mouth so that it moves when certain sounds are made;
- Tracing letters with fingers;
- Tapping out syllables.

How is multi-sensory teaching used to support children with learning difficulties?

It's generally accepted that a highly structured approach to support, utilising a variety of sensory stimulus, is an effective way to improve delayed literacy skills. Working one-to-one with a TA or teacher or in small groups on bespoke programmes has shown to improve the attainment of children who have struggled to make progress in a conventional whole class setting.

If a pupil is diagnosed with an SpLD, like dyslexia, the EP's report often makes reference to the provision of a personal plan and lessons of the kind described previously. These lessons have to be on a one-to-one or very small group basis as the aim is to address very specific gaps in knowledge and understanding; this usually includes a sharp focus on phonological knowledge, reading comprehension or handwriting. In these lessons, the TA or teacher very often uses a multi-sensory approach designed to stimulate the senses and enhance retention.

Various specialist teacher training courses which result in qualifications for TAs and teachers to work with pupils with SpLDs continue to promote a high level of personalisation. The post-graduate certificate (Level 5) course requires the teacher to design, develop and deliver a series of lessons in direct response to an ongoing process of assessment.

Good one-to-one teaching, whether delivered by a teacher or TA, is always carefully reviewed and needs to be based on very specific evidence about a child's prior learning. This kind of one-to-one teaching requires a great deal of time and effort in planning and review. It's often necessary to repeat and consolidate knowledge as progress may not be linear but very gradual, including steps back as well as steps forward. Making the process as multi-sensory as possible is another way of making something slow and meticulous, interesting and even fun.

Examples of multi-sensory approaches to teaching or reinforcing letter sounds might be; by using wooden letters which can be touched, held and rearranged by the pupil, or inviting a pupil to use a finger to draw the letter in a sand tray, whereby the teacher is deliberately introducing a specific sensory experience to focus and enhance a specific learning experience. Whether simply using colour in text or on cards, shaping numbers in putty or listening to a recording, the experience is designed to find a way to make a lasting impression on the pupil, to connect the knowledge to a sensory experience and, thereby, to fix it in the memory.

This type of teaching tends to take place in the context of an 'intervention', whether on a one-to-one basis or in a small group. The session is likely to take place in a space separate from the mainstream classroom. Even in well-resourced, new-build schools, the rooms used to provide this kind of specialist, multi-sensory tuition are generally the smaller classrooms, sometimes little more than cupboards and cubicles. They are, therefore, often spaces where it is easier to be selective about sensory input and to include stimuli by choice rather than by accident. This contrasts with the colour, light, sound, movement and frenetic activity that is the modern, mainstream classroom.

To be able to select and offer a specific sensory experience to support learning in the mainstream classroom, we need to be able to recognise and reduce sensory input as much as to select and include it.

Using the environment and avoiding distractions

Whilst it is becoming more common to see classrooms, even in primary settings that are less visually busy, most teaching rooms are still hugely stimulating to the senses. In primary settings especially, they are generally crammed with all the resources necessary to support a rich and varied curriculum. On one hand it's wonderful to see bustling and well-resourced spaces covered with the work, paintings and models made by the pupils, but for pupils with SEND and SpLDs, this presents a range of problems. Any kind of physical access issues tend to be more easily solved in clearer spaces; problems with cognition, memory and language also require attention to clarity: clarity of message, of language and of focus. The classroom needs to offer an environment for teaching that supports this. With the addition of washing lines hanging work, laptop cupboards, multiple and sometimes sliding boards on which there is text and colour, sound and language literally everywhere, it is perhaps not surprising that some pupils find it hard to find their way through learning; they can't see the forest for the trees.

Whilst the opportunities may be endless, making a good choice always involves narrowing the field.

It's generally true that primary classrooms tend to be rich in visual cues and secondary teaching rooms less so. However, being surrounded by visual cues is not the same as using them.

TAs can play an important role in making the classroom space more useful and less confusing for pupils with learning difficulties. One way to begin this process is by identifying and highlighting the various multi-sensory elements of the classroom.

Quite often, visual cues commonly found in the primary classroom disappear at Year 7 and a pupil might be too self-conscious to ask for it. This is a great chance for TAs to directly assist in enhancing the learning environment and providing a personalised toolbox for their learners. In the same way a TA might pre-teach content or vocabulary to prepare a pupil for a new aspect of the curriculum, in this model the TA prepares a child to get the best use out of their environment.

The TA points out the resource and explains it where necessary. The pupil is then asked to choose how they would like to access it, either as a feature common to all on the classroom wall or independently on request or from an accessible location.

The resources agreed as most useful might be located in a particular way, reproduced and then added to the planning for the class or pupils. The aim being that the pupil, teacher and the TA can optimise the use of the existing cues and have an opportunity to talk about and create additions and alternatives.

Common classroom resources may include:

- ✓ High frequency reference materials
- ✓ Key words
- ✓ Images
- ✓ Maps
- ✓ Diagrams
- ✓ Symbols and formulae
- ✓ Sentence starters
- ✓ Number line
- ✓ Clock face
- ✓ Tables square

- ✓ Literacy mat
- ✓ Numeracy mat
- ✓ Note-taking frame
- ✓ Writing frame
- ✓ Comprehension prompts (inference/main idea/facts etc.)
- ✓ Tablet/PC or other wireless devices

How can TAs help pupils with sensory needs to self-regulate in the classroom?

When even common occurrences like colour blindness or left-hand dominance are overlooked so frequently, it's important to recognise the importance of child-voice in adapting learning successfully. Sensory issues from hearing and visual impairments, to textural and colour preferences or aversions, can have a huge impact on a child's ability to focus on learning.

The audit in Table 4.1 can be used to have a focused discussion about the classroom environment and how it might affect pupils with SEND. It can be completed by any combination of TA, teacher or pupil, during or after a lesson.

Table 4.1 Sensory Audit of the Classroom/Teaching Space

Environment	Does this vary depending on the Activity?	How often does it vary?	Can this be improved?	Action
Lights: source & level				
Temperature				
Seating				
Space between furniture				
Height and angle of tables				
Use of headphones				
Orientation of room				
Air circulation				
Time spent in one attitude				
Seating plan				
View of the boards				
Access to basic materials				

What is a sensory diet?

Some pupils may have learning difficulties that are specific to sensory perception and reception. Those needing a high level of assistive technology and adaptation are likely to have been identified by the SENCO and assessed by specialists, who offer written and sometimes consultative advice to teachers and TAs.

However, other pupils whose primary needs may fall into one of the other categories (Cognition and Learning/Social, Emotional and Mental Health/ Speech Language and Communication) may also be more sensitive than usual to the sensory stimulus around them. This could include light, colour, heat, texture, pressure and even food and drink. Some of these pupils would benefit from a sensory diet made up of additional tools and activities to help them focus, concentrate and participate more fully.

Again, simple trial and error can be the best guide to supporting pupils who react adversely to everyday stimuli; it's helpful to have a 'sensory toolbox' on offer that includes:

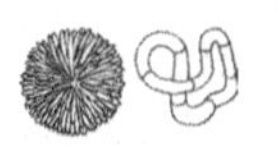

A variety of manipulatives like Koosh balls and tangles these can soothe and focus pupils who otherwise may seek sensory feedback by chewing sleeves or shredding books and paper or looking for spare equipment to manipulate;

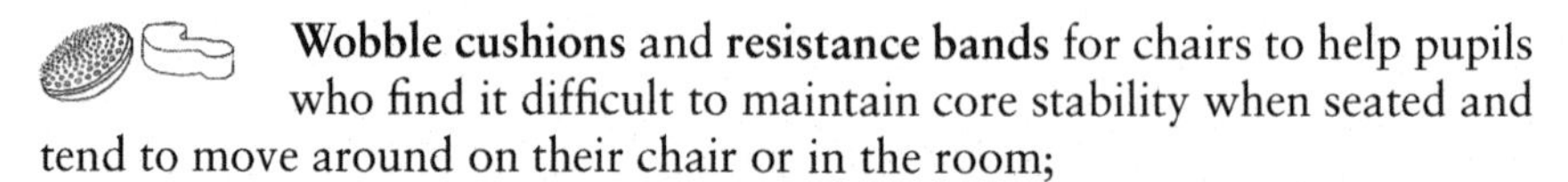

Wobble cushions and **resistance bands** for chairs to help pupils who find it difficult to maintain core stability when seated and tend to move around on their chair or in the room;

Grips for pens and pencils to make writing and drawing more comfortable;

Headphones which can be used to focus on recordings or excluding sound; and

Latex desk surfaces to grip paper and make writing and drawing more comfortable.

These individual measures can have significant and relatively instant impact and send a message that the classroom is an adaptable and welcoming place. If the teacher is able to participate and incorporate the use of such a tool themselves, this can help to normalise what might otherwise stand out as an adaptation. Unfortunately, as age and self-regulation can play a part in the successful use of these sensory aids, it does require a degree of practice and supervision on the part of the TA to ensure that pupils develop good habits. In secondary settings, these sensory aids might be necessary to find more mundane objects, as pupils become more sensitive to being different from their peers by using them. The message here though is not the sensory aid itself, but the purpose served.

Sensory cues and routines

Pupils are regularly expected to respond to sensory signals as triggers for transitions and routines. The way we think about these and consider varying them, the more we are able to include everyone. We are all used to the sound of the school bell, although often these days it is a more alarming 'boop' (often making visitors unused to the noise jump out of their skins). Reviewing signals and the routines they trigger can be a low cost and effective adjustment for pupils who may otherwise needed to be removed early or separated from a situation they find overwhelming or alarming.

TAs can offer helpful feedback by noticing the impact of sensory routines and cues on pupils they support. Making thoughtful decisions about these signals is in the interest of everyone, as it's usually possible to build in measures that make compliance easy and rule-breaking hard.

Table 4.2 identifies classroom routines, their potential impact on a pupil with sensory difficulties and some possible alternatives. It's helpful to complete the 'Impact on Pupil' column yourself following observation. The prompts in the box are just suggestions – all pupils are unique in this respect.

Table 4.2 Sensory Audit of Classroom Routines

Routine	Impact on Pupil	Possible adaptation
Lesson Change (bell)	Alarm, Crying, withdrawal, dawdling	Leave lesson early, Change seating, Use earphones, Change bell sound, Use Light, Use visual cue
Greeting	Cannot stand with others	Seated greeting
Standing and sitting in class	Finds it difficult to know when to stand and when to sit, may refuse to stand or sit as necessary	Rehearse expectations with pupil in advance, focus pupil on activity
Lining up for breaks	Upset by proximity to others	Provide rehearsal and regular place in line, either front or back, invite to line up in advance or last
Dressing for PE	Pupil struggles to dress, manage buttons and fastenings, laces and sequences	Pre-teach with visual cue cards showing process of dressing, simplify dress using velcro shoes, elastic tie. Etc.
Packing kit	Pupil. struggles to pack and unpack in time and good order, may forget items	Provide kit lists for each day of the week, encourage routines at school and home, rehearse, keep kit in one place

(*Continued*)

Table 4.2 (Continued)

Routine	Impact on Pupil	Possible adaptation
Collecting and depositing homework	Pupil may lose, forget and confuse homework materials and completed work	Provide a central place and a regular time and routine for handing in work, offer daily reminders on devices and diaries
Assembly	Pupil struggles with noise, number of people, volume of singing or time sitting	Sit near exit or TA, pre-teach routines including timing
Eating lunch	Pupil struggles with noise, food, cutlery, socialising	Alternate seating, timing, ear defenders, lunch buddy
Clearing up	Struggles to clear and tidy, movement around room distracting	Specific role in clearing, visual cues, pre-teaching
Registration time	Pupil does not respond to name	Verbal or physical signals
leaving a classroom	Pupil struggles to move on promptly or appropriately	Timed reminders counting down, clear routine for exit, accompanied transitions.
Breaks	Pupil may be isolated and unable to play or socialise successfully with peers	Establish safe place, activity, buddy, position of responsibility
Entering classroom	Pupil may be hesitant or disruptive on entering room	Greet outside room, rehearse expecations, first or last, allocated seating
Arriving at and leaving school	Pupil may be hesitant or reluctant to come to school or to leave	Designated person to greet each morning, escort, rehearsal day ahead or following day

What can I do to support pupils with specific triggers?

Some pupils, often those on the autistic disorder spectrum, have well-documented sensory triggers – everyday events or items as diverse as cardboard and *Doctor Who* can have a unique effect. Exposure to such triggers can create serious distress. Awareness of a child's history is helpful in avoiding this; however, it is possible that this response might arise in relation to triggers yet unknown. Only sensitivity and close attention to the diagnostic data, along with feedback from the child and from home, can effectively support a child in managing their response as they move through school.

What can I do to support pupils with visual and hearing impairments?

Most local authorities still employ specialists to support the inclusion of pupils with sensory impairment. It can be very helpful and informative to work alongside a specialist in visual or hearing impairments who can offer advice on practical matters. They can often offer TAs training and advice on the use of appropriate technology including radio-mics, laptops, or in making adaptations to or supplementing the materials for lessons.

Clearly, pupils with sensory impairments have very distinct and specific access issues and beyond that some will be more than able to manage the demands of school entirely independently and with great academic success. Making sure that they have a clear voice and role in planning and implementing useful support is essential.

Summary

How can TAs support multi-sensory teaching?

- Multi-sensory teaching addresses sight, sound, smell, taste and touch. This is designed to create a more memorable learning experience for pupils with learning difficulties.
- Successful one-to-one teaching is often characterised by careful planning, good evidence about prior knowledge and a multi-sensory approach to teaching.
- Small group and one-to-one teaching often takes place in spaces that are distinct and separate from the main classroom. These spaces benefit from being quieter and less visually distracting, allowing the teacher to include specific sensory stimulus to support the lesson.
- Classrooms can be distracting and over-stimulating for some students.
- It's useful to be aware of the visual cues and prompts available to support learning and to find out how useful they are to individual pupils.
- Creating a bespoke toolbox of items that supports independence in multi-sensory learning.
- It can be helpful to complete an audit of the teaching space and the way it is set up and used.
- Some pupils have specific sensory needs and require a sensory diet or access to resources to help them self-regulate and obtain sensory feedback when required to focus on learning.
- Routines and cues for transitions may require adaptation if all children are to be included in the mainstream classroom.
- It's important to be aware of specific triggers and to make a plan as to how these might be managed or avoided.
- Pupils with a hearing or visual impairment are often supported by a specialist who can offer advice to professionals about making adaptations to the curriculum and its delivery.

Resources

Table 4.1 Sensory Audit of the Classroom/Teaching Space

Environment	Does this vary depending on the Activity?	How often does it vary?	Can this be improved?	Action
Lights: source & level				
Temperature				
Seating				
Space between furniture				
Height and angle of tables				
Use of headphones				
Orientation of room				
Air circulation				
Time spent in one attitude				
Seating plan				
View of the boards				
Access to basic materials				

Table 4.2 Sensory Audit of Classroom Routines

Routine	Impact on Pupil	Possible Adaptation
Lesson change (bell)		
Greeting		
Standing and sitting in class		
Lining up for breaks		
Dressing for PE		
Packing kit		
Collecting and depositing homework		
Assembly		
Eating lunch		
Clearing up		
Registration time		
Leaving a classroom		
Breaks		
Entering classroom		
Arriving at and leaving school		

5 What is the role for TAs in supporting differentiation and adapting teaching?

This chapter introduces a series of light-hearted mnemonics referring to the seven most widely discussed routes into differentiation, and in doing so, clearly describes high quality, adaptive teaching. It explains that access to such teaching for pupils with SEND and SpLDs is often dependent on conscious adaptations to curriculum and delivery, including support and collaboration with TAs and effective interventions outside the classroom. This chapter describes a model for effective classroom support which enables pupils with SEND to access challenge, achievement and ultimately greater independence. A distinction is drawn between meeting educational needs and keeping SEND pupils on task and occupied.

Basis of this model

The model of in-class support presented in this chapter is mindful of the recommendations about good practice for TAs discussed in Chapter 2 and is dependent on an understanding of the 'core deficits' described in Chapter 3, namely:

- poor working memory
- poor phonological processing
- delayed processing time.

These deficits are most often linked to two categories of need as described in The Code: Cognition and Learning and Speech, Language and Communication Difficulties. However, the four categories of need (page 10) are not mutually exclusive. As previously mentioned, it is not impossible for pupils to have difficulties, and, therefore, educational needs related to more than one category. In fact, in our experience it is actually more likely that pupils experience a range of difficulties and have needs across the categories. It's worth remembering that we analyse difficulties, splitting them into different categories so we might understand their effects but, in doing this, we set up a false notion of what it is to be a child with SEND. A child's experience is integrated; all of their difficulties, and indeed, their abilities and talents occur together and, in that sense, are related. They experience classroom learning as a cocktail of demands and opportunities, each lesson a different set of ingredients, a different flavour and a different effect. What's more, pupils are usually unaware of the specific nature of their learning difficulties, other than the heightened frustration and anxiety they feel during the school day. What a teacher or TA might consider as different and problematic is actually the norm for the child who knows no different. For example, a child who finds instructions difficult to remember will perhaps only notice this as other pupils manage with greater ease, or as teachers move on and become impatient.

What are differentiation and adaptive teaching?

In order to address these 'core deficits', teachers and TAs are expected to differentiate and adapt teaching. Both sets of professional standards, for teachers and TAs, expect a level of knowledge in how to work with pupils to make changes to the learning experience that support access for all pupils including those with SEND.

The expectation is that effective differentiation enables teachers to meet the full range of learners' needs by using a range of strategies and adapted approaches. The ultimate aim is to ensure that ALL pupils have access to the most effective teaching and learning.

Historically, the aim was for 'gaps' to close and that pupils with learning difficulties would progress and attain in line with their peers. However, it's likely that progression for children with learning difficulties may be a slow and uneven path. This is now recognised in the new inspection framework; 'the provider has the same academic, technical or vocational ambitions for almost all learners. Where this is not practical – for example, for some learners with high levels of SEND – its curriculum is designed to be ambitious and to meet their needs' (Education Inspection Framework (EIF), 2020).

Determining appropriate expectations and accurate predictions for pupils with learning difficulties requires a degree of thoughtful consideration. Keeping aspirations high, and not confusing literacy and numeracy with other indicators of intelligence, is vital; there is more than one way into learning and a million and one possibilities for success.

Differentiation and adapting teaching can work in two stages. To differentiate is to acknowledge and to try to understand the differences between one pupil and another. To successfully adapt teaching is to take the appropriate action to ensure that difference does not necessarily become disadvantage or reduce challenge, aspiration and achievement.

Clearly, a learning difficulty by definition can create a divide between the pupil and academic success, slowing progress and limiting attainment. Effective differentiation must acknowledge the difficulties pupils face with the curriculum and adaptation should help to create a way through it. Best practice can encourage pupils to use their abilities to overcome the barriers to learning they face.

It's important to recognise that sometimes in our haste to identify and deal with problems, we can overlook the fact that children with learning difficulties are also children with learning abilities. One does not cancel out the other. In fact, when learning difficulties are specific, contrasting and distinct strengths and weaknesses are a commonplace characteristic.

Recognition of pupil ability, interest, curiosity and motivation is pivotal in building the resilience needed to progress. Differentiation should not be designed to occupy, pacify or placate pupils but rather to engage them in learning and to motivate them to achieve.

Meeting SEND does not mean removing challenge from the curriculum. Meeting needs means understanding the nature of the challenge for the individual child; it means appropriate challenge. Without some consideration of appropriate challenge, school becomes a disheartening, repetitive slog for the pupil (and for the professionals).

How do teachers differentiate and adapt teaching?

The approach offered here is based on best practice for differentiation and adaptation. It's taken from my first book, *Effective Differentiation* (Gray, 2018) and is adapted from the model described in Jayne Bartlett's book *Outstanding Differentiation for Learning in the Classroom* (Bartlett, 2016).

Effective differentiation can only be achieved if knowledge becomes practice, and practice informs knowledge. Our aim is to enhance the effectiveness of classroom teaching by reflecting on practice and optimising its effect, without the need for expensive additional resources, acknowledging that in-class support is only a part of the jigsaw puzzle of SEND provision. Schools require continued support, resources and training in meeting the needs of their pupils. The following pages describe differentiation and adaptation as a refinement of teaching that can be embedded into daily practice for teachers and the TAs that support them.

It's about thinking differently and acting thoughtfully.

DR GOPTA is an acronym that helps teachers and TAs to remember seven ways to differentiate and adapt teaching. It sets out an agenda to enhance access to the curriculum for pupils with SEND and SpLDs.

Each letter of **DR GOPTA** stands for a way to support a child who is struggling with their learning.

D	Dialogue	Adapting classroom talk
R	Resources	Providing alternative, supplementary materials and tools
G	Grouping	Creating supportive partnerships
O	Outcome	Offering alternative ways to show knowledge and understanding
P	Pace	Changing timelines for success
T	Task	Adapting activities
A	Assessment	Making the most of feedback

The aim of the **DR GOPTA** agenda is to adapt teaching, differentiate and to ensure pupils with SEND access the best possible teaching and learning experience. Research has shown that to learn effectively and progress at school all pupils need daily opportunities to:

M	Make Links	connect learning and experiences
R	Take Risks	learn to fail, recover and try again
C	Engage Cognitively	think and remember
H	Think at a Higher Level	think critically, practically, creatively and analytically
U	Check Understanding	avoid misunderstanding
F	Share Feedback	clear, helpful information sharing
I	Be Independent	to work without support

We call this the **MR CHUFI** agenda; it sits alongside **DR GOPTA**, two memorable characters that create a framework for *how* and *why* to differentiate and adapt teaching for pupils with SEND and SpLDs.

How do DR GOPTA and MR CHUFI help TAs to support pupils?

In most educational research models, differentiation and adaptation are assumed to be led by teachers. As we already know, The Code promotes an essential role of the classroom teacher in leading learning for all children. However, our observation (over the last couple of decades) is that TAs often take an absolutely central role in this process.

Let's think about some of the **DR GOPTA** activities TAs engage in every day:

- ✓ TAs prompt children and talk them through their work (**D**);
- ✓ TAs make or find resources (**R**);
- ✓ TAs work in groups (**G**);
- ✓ TAs suggest alternative outcomes (**O**);
- ✓ TAs break things down and change the pace (**P**);
- ✓ TAs alter the task to assist the pupils (**T**);
- ✓ TAs offer feedback and get involved in assessment (**A**).

TAs can find themselves acting responsively and helping pupils to complete tasks rather than proactively supporting pupils to develop skills and strategies to cope independently. The over-arching aim is for the child to take part in activities, to 'keep up' with their peers, to be on task or to behave co-operatively. The more beneficial learning focus of **MR CHUFI** is overlooked. 'Doing' trumps 'thinking'. Cognitive engagement can be overshadowed by task completion.

With this is mind, we have aimed to devise a structure for TAs to inform classroom practice. It brings together the **DR GOPTA and MR CHUFI** agendas; effective differentiation for effective learning. The new agenda acknowledges the unique position of TAs, its opportunities and limitations.

Meet **DR KEEPIT**.

DR KEEPIT is a single checklist that anyone can easily remember and refer to when faced with a SEND challenge in the classroom.

DR GOPTA + MR CHUFI ⇨ DR KEEPIT

It's a list made in the light of all the received wisdom covered in the previous chapters and allows the most inexperienced TA access to the insights of the most experienced. The best solutions often don't require rocket science, just well-informed common sense (which we find TAs have in abundance).

DR KEEPIT draws together both a rationale and some key activities to consider when providing support to pupils in the classroom. It's flexible enough to include pupils with SEND in any and all categories of need.

This chapter takes each of the letters in turn and offers suggestions and activities that illustrate how to apply it to everyday life in school.

This system is designed to benefit the pupil and to:

- ✓ increase pupil progress and attainment
- ✓ achieve better pupil and staff well-being
- ✓ develop pupil voice
- ✓ increase attendance
- ✓ improve behaviour
- ✓ increase participation.

DR KEEPIT is designed to put the child at the centre of the learning experience, so with the TA's help, they are more likely to hold onto the knowledge they gain in class – they literally **KEEPIT**.

Note: The order of the letters is to aid memory by creating a word, *not* to suggest the priority or the order in which the features should be used.

D	Dialogue	Adapting classroom talk
R	Resources	Providing alternative, supplementary materials and tools
K	Key Points learning	Promoting a focus on learning objectives
E	Engagement and participation	Promoting focus on thinking
E	Encouragement and motivation	Promoting a positive attitude to school – a healthy approach to feedback
P	Proximity	Promoting independence
I	Identifying barriers	Being alert to the impact of learning difficulties
T	Task chunking	Adapting the pace of learning, 'breaking it down'

DIALOGUE

Adapting Classroom Talk

Why should TAs adapt dialogue?

Adapting classroom talk is possibly one of the least time-consuming and most powerful opportunities for TAs and teachers to enhance their practice and have greater impact. It's almost impossible to think about a model of in-class support that doesn't rely on regular verbal or indeed signed communication between TA and pupil. Having said that, a sustained criticism of generalised in-class support has been that it can shut down rather than open up useful conversations about learning.

To make the most of these conversations, it's important to be clear about three things; their purpose, their content and their form. A thoughtful approach to how we talk with pupils, what we say and when we say it, is more likely to develop a child's knowledge and skills and, above all, foster greater independence in learning.

The TA very often acts as a filter for classroom language, listening out for information and instructions, repeating and paraphrasing the teacher's words. This places TAs in the middle of a chain of communication. How you approach this and what you choose to say to a pupil can have a profound effect on their access to the lesson. It's possible to use this opportunity to support effective teaching and learning by helping pupils to: **M**ake Links, Take **R**isks, Engage **C**ognitively, Think at a **H**igher Level, Check **U**nderstanding, Share **F**eedback and Be **I**ndependent (**MR CHUFI**).

It's also possible to miss this opportunity and take over, taking the lead on learning and undertake the **MR CHUFI** agenda in the child's place. This may mean the child finishes the lesson with a completed task but unless the child has done at least one or two of the **MR CHUFI** activities themselves, it's unlikely that they will have made much progress in terms of their own knowledge and understanding.

Adapting dialogue to support 'core deficits'

Working memory

Poor working memory has an important part to play when considering classroom conversations with pupils. A word to the wise; less is more. Remember that working memory is one of the three core deficits we address in Chapter 3. In their book *The Working Memory Advantage*, Alloway and Alloway (2013) explore the impact of working memory on all aspects of learning. They describe working memory as the brain's 'conductor'. This conductor works hard to retain, prioritise and process information – to 'do something with the information at hand rather than just remember it briefly' (Alloway & Alloway, 2013, p. 8). One aspect of working memory is the 'phonological loop'. It acts like a reel of audio tape in the brain that stores spoken and written material. If a child has a poor working memory, this loop may fail and as a consequence they are likely to forget instructions or key information. This can affect their ability to tackle their work; as they struggle to keep the instructions **in mind**, while trying to recall important information (prior knowledge), and then focus on what might need to be done to complete the task at hand.

Phonological processing

It's also possible that alongside a poor working memory, pupils experience difficulty in processing speech sounds (phonological processing) and have completely missed, forgotten or confused key words or sounds. If these two problems occur in tandem, they have a 'double whammy' effect that seriously impairs a child's ability to manage verbal instructions and information.

The demands of the mainstream classroom in this respect can be entirely overwhelming.

A TA with some specific awareness of a child's specific difficulties has an opportunity to ensure a clear message is received and mistakes corrected. It may be that diagnostic material exists that identifies these problems. Some children struggle with specific sounds or blends, and some have problems hearing the initial, medial or final sound; think of the difference in meaning between 'bend', 'bent', 'bendy' and 'bends'. Prefixes and suffixes also have a significant impact on meaning think of, 'usage', 'uses', 'useful', 'useless'. Unless you can identify all of the sounds, the meaning of a sentence can be lost.

Processing time

It's vital for TAs, and indeed for teachers, to be aware of their pace of speech when introducing, discussing and instructing. Teachers and TAs are often confident speakers who use language with ease and enthusiasm. When we speak too quickly and constantly re-phrase our message, we disadvantage our pupils. Pupils with SEND may well have great difficulty identifying the important information from a continuous stream of teacher talk. When teachers talk to the class, it's possible that they share all kinds of information: explanations, instructions, details, questions and even jokes and asides. In the same way that people often re-read a page of dense text to decipher its meaning, a pupil who struggles with processing and remembering speech may feel just as lost when listening.

This places a responsibility on TAs and teachers to be aware of their pace of speech and to recognise that less is sometimes more. Pupils might be wrongly accused of simply 'not listening' when actually they listened to every word but didn't have the capacity to process and retain the important parts of what had been said.

How can TAs adapt the dialogue?

The first step to having more effective conversations with pupils is to reflect on your own practice and establish what happens now.

As TAs and teachers are seldom recorded and relatively rarely observed, it's tricky to be objective about your own classroom language. There are a couple of options for this; it is possible to use the 'Classroom Talk Audit' (Table 5.1).

This is a simple checklist to be used for reflection on existing habits when talking to pupils in class. It lists a number of ways we use language in supporting teaching. The terms are explained in grey, where necessary, and we have included one or two examples to get started.

Table 5.1 Classroom Talk Audit

Closed questions	
Open questions	
Instructions	
Praise words	
Pupils praised	
Reprimands	
Students sanctioned	
Checking understanding	
Pauses for thought	
Encouraging speech	
Grammar in speech	
Position when talking	
Repetition	
Managing misunderstanding	
Varying tone, volume and register	
Clarity of speech (staff)	
Pace of speech	

TAs could make a recording of themselves working with a pupil (with the necessary permissions) or they could invite a colleague to observe them.

Or

TAs could use the audit as a self-reflection to think through existing habits.

Whichever TAs choose, the aim is to develop a greater self-awareness about the way language is currently used and its impact on your pupils.

We have set out the format so that it can be edited and used to do one or more of the following:

✓ to tally up how many times something is said in a lesson;
✓ to record some of the actual words and phrases used to manage every-day situations.

Reflecting on feedback

Once the TA has completed an audit, the feedback should provide some useful insights into their existing use of talk. A TA may wish to repeat the audit to compare language in different lessons, and with different pupils, to get an even better picture.

Interpreting the audit with pupils can help to build a pupil's self-awareness and help them to make more conscious choices about classroom language.

Closed and open questions

Before asking a question we really need to have some idea of what kind of opportunity it is designed to create. Open and closed questions present pupils with very different approaches to tasks in terms of thinking and processing. Closed questions tend to be answered quickly (or skipped over) and open questions can create a pause that might feel uncomfortable; this is because they often require more time for thinking. In any lesson it's likely that both kinds of questions need to be asked for a variety of purposes. The important thing is that there is some variety and some challenge for the pupil. It's important to have some open questions in our tool belt that we can use to create a conversation about learning (see Resource One at the end of this chapter). It's also important that we are prepared to wait, listen and encourage pupils in providing their answer. See **Engagement** for a more detailed discussion about how to listen actively and to develop a pupil's ability to listen actively (page X).

Instructions

It might be that instructions form the majority of classroom talk. It's impossible to identify whether the tally of how many instructions there are is enough for a typical lesson; it might have been necessary to repeat or to break instructions into smaller steps, effectively creating more instructions. The key reflection is to think about the quality and effectiveness of instructions. If a child is failing to follow instructions or remember them and needs constant reminders, it might be helpful to ask yourself three questions. Are instructions:

- explicit and distinct from other classroom talk?
- displayed visually or in symbols?
- using a vocabulary that the pupil understands?

More information about giving instructions effectively is in **Key Points** on page 71.

Praise words

Hopefully, in the audit, the TA is able to identify the language they use to praise, how often they currently use it and the effect it has on the pupil. Do they work harder, show pride and thank you or do they shy away and look downcast? If a TA wants to encourage a child to progress, to be more independent in their learning and to succeed at school, it's proven to be more fruitful to praise specific actions, attitudes and accomplishments rather than praise the child as a whole. If you would like some support in developing this, go to the section on **Encouragement** on page 84.

Pupils praised

Does your feedback and praise extend beyond the identified pupils you support?

Reprimands

If a child has broken a rule and the TA wants to acknowledge this and take some action, they may well have standard phrases to use. Like praise, it's important to use language that keeps the focus on the rule breaking, not the child. Being explicit about what you want to see supports a consistent and respectful approach. Most schools have complex behaviour management policies in place that identify language and processes. Make sure you have seen and read this advice.

Students sanctioned

Does a TA's authority extend to give sanctions of some kind? Are you clear about who you are able to sanction and how?

Checking understanding

A great deal of a TA's working life is dedicated to checking pupil's understanding of the lesson content and activities. However, it's important to draw a clear distinction between checking that a pupil knows what to do, and checking a pupil's understanding of what is being taught. If the focus falls on what to do next, lessons can become training sessions in appearing to learn, coping with the activities and finding a way to pass through school unnoticed. This issue is dealt with in more detail in the next section on **Key Points** on page 71.

Pauses for thought

Making sure TAs pause and allow pupils to think gets overlooked. We like to live in a world where content is instantaneous, and we can get irritated very quickly by that little 'buffering' symbol often seen on computers. Pupils with learning difficulties need more time than most, so we have to become comfortable with making time for thinking and allowing silence.

How can I encourage pupils to speak?

Sometimes pupils with SEND can be reluctant to join in the classroom conversation. When pupils have more significant difficulties with speech production and articulation, it is likely that technology or alternative systems of communications are being used (alternative and augmentative communication or AAC). This may include pictures, gestures, sign language, visual aids or speech-output devices like computers. Any TA expected to use such means would need to take part in a specific programme of training.

Pupils with SpLDs might struggle to participate actively and successfully for many reasons, such as lack of vocabulary or problems in constructing a sentence or a question. If they have to wait for more than a few seconds, they might find it hard to remember what they want to say. They might find it hard to focus on the topic or read the materials. It may just be too big a risk to their delicate self-esteem. It shouldn't surprise us when the same reluctance is often expressed by adults, even seasoned professionals, who feel shy when asking a question in a meeting. Asking a question is a basic expression of vulnerability; it draws attention to something you don't know or have misunderstood. Children with SEND are more vulnerable in this respect than their non-SEND peers. Effective TAs have a sense of empathy for their pupils and can develop effective and sensitive ways of bringing their voice into the classroom conversation.

This is made even more important in the context of recent research into the negative impact of smart phone culture on family life. It is clear, at the school gate and beyond, that we are spending more and more time engaged with our devices, perusing menus of tailor-made enticements. This is time we are not spending talking, in person, to each other. It would seem that the classroom offers a unique opportunity for children to explore conversation in a device-free space, a space where the focus is entirely on them. Therefore, it is essential that TAs be vigilant and ensure that school age children with SEND and SpLDs have the best possible opportunity to participate. This means being regularly and actively encouraged to speak.

> 'Asking a question is a basic expression of vulnerability, it draws attention to something you don't know or have misunderstood.'

Grammar in speech

It's amazing how many adults, including teachers, tilt their heads quizzically at this one. Grammar seems to be more often associated with writing than with language in general. Whether writing or speaking, grammar is the system; it describes the conventions we use to create meaning with words.

The reflection here is simple: are we modelling the system that children are expected to use in their speech and writing?

Position when talking

For TAs, this is examined in more detail in **Proximity** on page 92. However, it is useful to note and to think about how a pupil's response varies depending on the locations of the speaker. Do children turn or move to see and find the speaker, and does this have an effect on their response or attention? It's also interesting to note how a pupil responds to audio only sources, where the speaker cannot be seen at all.

Repetitions

This is an interesting tally to compare across a number of different lessons. Does it vary and what's the reason? Is there an easier way to prompt remembering the 'less is more' rule?

Managing misunderstanding

When pupils have misunderstood, forgotten or make an error, what do we say? Acknowledging errors is obviously important; however, it is possible to do so in a constructive and non-judgemental way. It may well be true that we learn more from our errors than our successes, but in order for our pupils to do so, we need to maintain their motivation and self-esteem.

Variation of volume, tone and register

Children need experience of all the ways we use our voices if they are to develop good social language skills. Are we modelling appropriate volume, and do we make sure our tone fits our purpose and do we modify our language to suit the situation?

Clarity of speech

Do we speak clearly enough to be understood?

Pace of speech

See **Processing Time** earlier. Pace not only impacts how much of the language we understand and can recall, but it all conveys attitude and sometimes emotion. When we listen to different speakers, does their pace of speech have an impact on our attitude to listening?

Providing Alternative and Supplementary Materials and Tools

Why should TAs adapt resources?

It seems important to acknowledge that resources to support pupils with SEND extends beyond the provision of alternative and supplementary materials and tools. Everything with a cost attached that is used to provide support and adapt teaching, including staff time, is a resource. Human resources can be difficult to quantify and apportion but it's worth noting that the vast majority of a school budget is spent on its staff. Getting the best value for money from the human, technical and material resources we have is essential if provision is to be efficient and effective.

Before adapting resources and providing additional, supplementary materials and tools, it's important to be clear about what is already available in classrooms, stock cupboards and on servers and to make sure these are being used effectively.

Obviously, some resources are abundant and available to *all* members of the class, and others might be limited for the use of a particular pupil or group of pupils. In addition to this, there may be resources (material, technological and curricular) specifically to be used with pupils with SEND as part of their special educational provision – i.e. which are considered 'additional to' and 'different from' (The Code, 2015) the standard classroom offer.

Resources that support specific 'core deficits'

When thinking about resources and the most effective way to use them, it is always a good idea to start with the pupil. By starting with the pupil and thinking about the impact of their underlying difficulties: working memory, phonological processing and processing speed, and then also considering any sensory needs, the TA can make an informed choice in finding alternatives and adaptations to help remove their barriers to learning.

In the following pages we have identified and explained *some* of the most useful and widely available resources. For each core deficit we have focused on some material resources and then a suggested technological resource. We consider these to be the essentials.

Each pupil is unique; there can't be a 'one size fits all' approach to adapting resources. Instead, it is more of a 'trial and error' process with the child, where they, too, have a voice. It is important to include the child when selecting resources as they need to feel comfortable and confident in using them in front of their peers. There is some skill involved in managing this negotiation as a pupil may need some encouragement and support in trying new things.

Resources for pupils with poor working memory

The mini-whiteboard

The mini-whiteboard is one of the most common resources in classrooms, especially in Primary settings, and it's not unheard of in Secondary schools. Some teachers delight in using them regularly in their teaching; all pupils are often familiar and confident in their use. Pupils particularly enjoy that what they write is a draft, it's temporary and *not* the finished article. This provides an element of freedom for children as presentation is not at issue, work can be erased quickly, and it can be more enjoyable to write with a board pen rather than a normal pen or pencil. It is also becoming more common in schools to find 'whiteboard' style desks which work in the same way as the mini-whiteboard and allow pupils to write directly onto the table!

How it can be used

The mini-whiteboard is a great resource for TAs to have at hand. For pupils with poor working memory, it provides an immediate visual aid that can act as a reminder for instructions and information presented verbally. This key information, so often forgotten, can be temporarily recorded with words, pictures or symbols. Whilst the TA could offer to do the recording initially, the intention would be that the pupil could make their own memory prompts on the mini- whiteboard whilst proactively engaged in listening. This practice supports a metacognitive approach to learning, helping the pupil to understand how well their memory works and how much information they are able to recall from what they have heard.

The mini-whiteboard can also be used to record a *process*; the steps involved in undertaking a task. Pupils with poor working memory often struggle with sequencing, for example, days of the week, seasons, lessons in a day, prime numbers, months of the year, etc.; and ordering of information. By using the mini-whiteboard, pupils are able to erase each step of the task as they complete it, thereby supporting effective planning in producing a piece of work.

Sticky notes and tabs

Sticky notes are an easy and accessible resource for pupils of all ages. They come in a variety of colours and sizes which makes them even more appealing for pupils to use. They are a great kinesthetic tool for sequencing. The manual movement of sticking and re-sticking illustrates a pupil's thought process in a physical and visual way.

How they can be used

Sticky notes can be used in a variety of ways to aid a poor working memory. They can be attached to any text, exercise books, textbooks, work sheets or even computer screens. Their use can be modelled by the TA:

To help with organisation

* To jot down key words, instructions and reminders.
* To 'chunk tasks' into smaller pieces.
* To establish a chronological or logical order. This is particularly useful for pupils who struggle to sequence tasks and often only remember the last instruction that they hear.
* To record a sequence of instructions or steps.
* To prompt regarding time.
* To offer praise or feedback.

Planning a written response

Pupils with poor working memory often struggle to organise their thoughts for longer pieces of writing, whether that be in creating stories or descriptive pieces in primary school or writing essays and extended answers in secondary school. Sticky notes offer a quick and easy way for a child to plan; each idea captured on a separate note, and then moved around to create the structure for their writing. If they change their mind, or find new information, they can add in additional thoughts or remove ideas before they start to write whole sentences and paragraphs.

Mind-mapping software

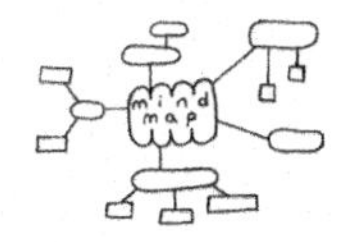

Mind-mapping is a visual way of organising information. A variety of pictures, symbols, diagrams or words can be used to capture the thinking that goes on inside a pupil's head. There is no set order or pattern to follow. It is a colourful and creative way to literally 'map out' a pupil's ideas as they happen. There are also a number of mind-mapping packages (e.g. MindView, Inspiration, Popplet) available that allow a pupil to perform this process on a device or computer. These computer packages or apps can sometimes be free to use, although with most, a subscription is required. Some schools may have a whole-school subscription to a mind-mapping package which is installed on classroom computers, and so it would be helpful to have a conversation with the ICT co-ordinator.

How it can be used

Pupils with poor working memory may struggle to keep hold of their ideas, which may occur very quickly and at the same time, rather than in a linear sequence. Mind-mapping software provides easy to use 'thought-bubbles' which the child can fill instantly, thinking about order or connections later. The map can then act as a tool to prompt additional thoughts or development of those ideas. One of the advantages of using mind-mapping online, rather than on a mini-whiteboard or piece of paper, is the repositioning and reordering feature. This helps pupils to make connections and prioritise, creating a structure for their response. Mind-mapping software also allows pictures and photos to be inserted and saved. This is a quick way to retain a thought which can be revisited at any future point. Some packages even turn the visual mind map into a list which further aids pupils in their writing. Mind-mapping software is a fun and easy tool to help pupils with SEND to structure, organise and recall their thoughts.

***Resources for pupils with poor* phonological processing**

Reference materials such as phonic grids, word lists and subject specific vocabulary are usually widely available from the internet or in your setting. These resources are helpful for children who struggle with spelling and reading which are most commonly impacted by this 'core deficit'.

This can prevent pupils from getting stuck at the phonological processing stage in their reading. Additional resources can enable them to overcome this barrier to their learning and allow them to complete the task more easily.

There is sometimes an objection raised against using these resources because they cannot be taken into exams or used in test situations. However, if a pupil 'sees' the graphemes for sounds, key words or subject specific vocabulary every day in front of them, there is a greater chance that they will remember and embed some, or most, of these sounds or words into their long-term memory. This should increase their vocabulary knowledge and provide them with more confidence in their spelling and reading.

- **Diphthong**: a single sound formed by the combination of two **vowels** in a syllable – 'oa' as in boat, 'ea' as in feat.
- **Phoneme**: distinct unit of sound in a specific language; English has 44 phonemes but 26 letters.
- **Grapheme**: a letter or a number of letters that represent a sound (phoneme) in a word. This might be a single letter or a number of letters, e.g. *igh* in night.
- **Digraph**: a combination of two **letters** representing a single sound *ay* as in day, *ph* as in photo.

It also helps to prevent those situations where a pupil can find and say a word but avoid writing it because they struggle with spelling. This practice often means poor spelling masks underlying ability across a range of subjects. Providing such materials can help pupils link sounds to letters and encourage pupils to use the correct vocabulary in their writing. This demonstrates the vocabulary which matches their true level of understanding and knowledge.

Phonic grids provide a visual representation of all of the letters in the alphabet which make similar sounds. They are freely available on the internet and come in a variety of colours and sizes. They are a visual aid to support phonological knowledge.

Phonic grids are more commonly used in primary schools, and particularly in Reception and KeyStage 1. However, for a pupil with SEND and a specific 'core deficit' in phonological processing, having access to a phonic grid in Keystage 2, and even in Secondary school, can boost their confidence in spelling and reading.

Key word lists may be relevant to a particular task, high frequency words, or simply a personalised list of words that pupils struggle to remember and use correctly. It might be possible to offer these in a variety of forms. Words may be written in a list with an explanation or, perhaps, segmented by the use of colour to identify the phonemes. Again, this is a process of trial and error and dependent on noticing what works for the pupil.

Subject specific vocabulary lists identify important words that have a high frequency in a subject area. They may consist of technical vocabulary which can be irregular in spelling and have more than three syllables, e.g. '*photosynthesis*'. However, trickier still are homonyms which have the same spelling and pronunciation but different meanings in different subjects, e.g. product, range, sphere, medium, content, table, etc.

How they can be used

Phonic grids, key word lists and subject specific vocabulary should be easily accessible and close to the pupil whilst they are working.

If a child is struggling to spell a word, they can use the phonic grid to find the possible letter combinations for the sounds in that word; they can then make a best guess or check in with the TA that their selection is correct.

These can be written on anything; a mini-whiteboard, in their own personalised vocabulary booklet, on sticky notes or tabs, on a bookmark, on a desk in a classroom, on the wall, on coloured cards, on tracing paper slotted inside the book – as long as the words are accessible and available.

Reading rulers and highlighter pens

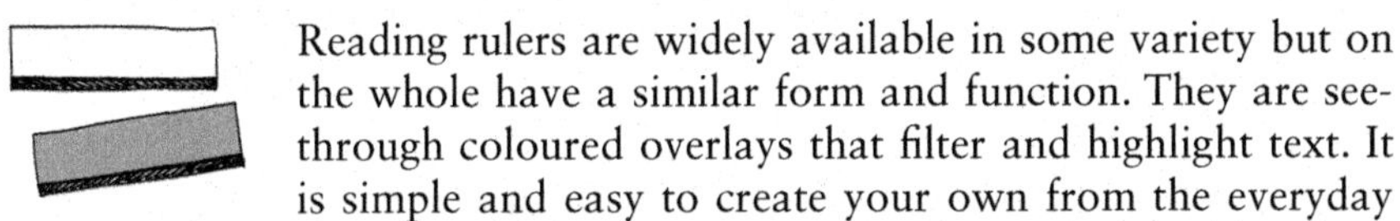

Reading rulers are widely available in some variety but on the whole have a similar form and function. They are see-through coloured overlays that filter and highlight text. It is simple and easy to create your own from the everyday resources that are around you in schools. Reading rulers generally provide two specific functions: to ensure that pupils track the words across a line in a clear way; and to reduce contrast and distortion and improve the experience of reading black print on a white surface.

Visual tracking: the ability to efficiently move the eyes from left to right (or right to left, up and down, and circular motions) OR focusing on an object as it moves across a person's **visual** field.

How they can be used

Pupils with poor phonological processing skills can often find the whole experience of reading slow, difficult and painful. The aim of the reading ruler is to try and reduce visual stress. The ruler should be placed under the line of text and moved down the page as the child is reading. This also serves the function of chunking the amount of reading into manageable sections. This can also be achieved by simply using a folded piece of paper (landscape) and using this as a makeshift reading ruler. Blocking out text, other than the immediate, prevents the pupil from subconsciously focusing on the challenge ahead or the sheer volume of words. By moving the sheet of paper down the page as they read each line, the child is often surprised by how quickly they have read the whole text.

For some pupils, and indeed adults, reading black text on a white background can be a strain to the eyes because of the stark contrast between the two colours. If a child has only ever read text that is black on white, then they may not realise that a different combination of colours may make reading easier on the eye. Some children may see letters 'dancing' around on the page, words distorted or words with shadows behind them. It is not until they see words that are not black text on a white background that they realise words are indeed fixed on a page clearly. Specialist dyslexic reading rulers come in a range of colours and children are encouraged to place these over the words that they are reading. However, this can be easily replicated with a piece cut from a clear plastic coloured folder, or alternatively by photocopying text onto a piece of coloured paper. Before doing this, it might be worth experimenting with a child to see if colour makes a difference to their reading, by writing some sentences for them to read on a coloured piece of paper with a blue or green pen. If this makes the words significantly easier to read, then pursuing the coloured overlay alternatives for reading would be helpful. The child may need a specific Visual Stress Test which can be carried out by an optometrist. Not every child experiences a benefit from coloured overlays or coloured paper.

Highlighter pens

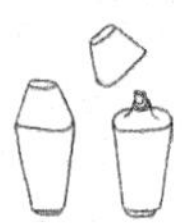

Highlighter pens are used to illuminate and draw focus to specific words in a text.

How they can be used

Children with a 'core deficit' of phonological processing will take longer, and use more effort, to decode the words that they are reading. As the focus will be on reading the word, often the meaning and context of a word is lost or forgotten. Children regularly have to re-read the passage or text when they get to the end and have to answer questions about it.

Therefore, teaching children to read with a highlighter pen in their hand is a really useful skill. When they are reading, they should be encouraged to stop at every full stop, go back over the sentence and highlight key words only. Using different colours to highlight words and collate evidence will aid their understanding of what they are reading. Once the text has been read, then the colour-highlighted words should help to reduce the volume of information to the key points and will help guide the child quickly back to just the text that is useful and relevant for completing the task. They may need to re-read these words again, but this will be far fewer than having to re-read the whole passage. If a pupil is having to read from a text book, highlighting is obviously not an option, but where possible and if there is a substantial quantity to read, the TA can always photocopy one or two pages from a book so that the child is able to highlight and colour-code information in the same way.

Reading pens and computer readers

Two of the most commonly used technological resources for children with poor phonological processing are reading pens and computer readers.

The reading pen is a small scanning device which is held like a pen. The pupil can roll the pen across a piece of text and when they lift the pen from the page, it reads aloud the words that have just been scanned. It can be connected to headphones, which means it can be used in a classroom or exam environment without disturbing others in the room. There are some pens which also have a built-in dictionary, but these are not allowed in exams or tests. Reading pens are expensive, but they do provide a level of independence to the pupil who has poor phonological processing, and if used effectively, can help to remove this barrier to their learning.

A computer reader acts in a similar way to a reading pen, in that the text is read aloud on a computer screen to the pupil. 'Immersive reader' is a tool that is available across all platforms of Microsoft Office, including Microsoft Edge, which is an internet browser.

How they can be used

If reading pens are used in classroom practice currently, they can be used in external examinations to support children with identified reading difficulties. As the device reads the words in a monotone voice and no meaning can be implied through intonation, this use extends to include tests of reading where a person acting as a reader is not allowed.

A computer reader offers a number of possibilities. If a child is researching information on the internet, they are able to use the 'immersive reader' tool and have that information read to them whilst each word is highlighted on the page. This resource can also be helpful for listening to a class text through audio books as there are many available online. Like the reading pen, the computer reader can be used in exams and can read any PDF version of an exam paper, which can be pre-ordered by the school from the examination boards. The child is able to wear headphones to listen to the paper being read aloud, although they would need access to a computer rather than just being able to sit in a normal classroom or exam hall, which is the advantage of using a reading pen.

Resources for pupils with slow processing speeds

Slow processing speeds can relate to a variety of different areas that then affect a pupil's ability to perform a task at speed. In mathematics and English this can manifest itself in a pupil not able to recall their times tables quickly enough, or to recall a word that they wish to use in their writing. All the resources mentioned thus far are useful to support this issue. However, the only really valid resource for this underlying need is time itself. Finding ways to use the other resources that allow pupils time to process and to revisit information and instructions is the key here. Having said that, pupils with SEND often struggle to have a clear concept of 'time' and may not be able to judge the difference between 5 minutes and 15 minutes; they may not know what time 'feels' like.

Clocks and timers

Timers of various kinds may be useful in allowing pupils to develop greater awareness of the passage of time, whilst acting as a prompt to begin or move on in a task. There are a range of timers that visually show the passage of time in different ways. Obviously, clocks and stopwatches indicate the passage of time, but a number of alternatives exist to represent this visually. These include time shown as a block of colour or, indeed, grains of sand that visually diminish can be very useful for children who also struggle with a conventional watch or clock.

Touch-typing

Slow speed of handwriting can have a significant effect on a pupil when they are performing daily classroom tasks. The emphasis on the importance of neat and legible cursive script is a key assessment objective in Keystage 1 and continues to be assessed formally in Keystage 2. For this reason, there are numerous handwriting intervention schemes available for primary age children who are regularly encouraged to improve their written presentation skills. However, for pupils who have a SEND, the physical process of writing can be uncomfortable and cognitively draining. They may spend their focus and concentration on letter formation or letter presentation rather than on what it is they wish to write.

Touch-typing is often considered the most productive way to produce work as it not only alleviates the manual process of writing but can also enable pupils to reorganise ideas and paragraphs and support sequencing and organisation. Learning to touch-type requires pupils to train their muscle memory to locate the letters on the keyboard, allowing them to type using all of their fingers, without having to look at the keys. This is particularly helpful if a child is making notes from the whiteboard, as it minimises the process of having to look at the board and then look down at their work and prevents them from forgetting the information they have just seen during this very simple action. However, efficient touch-typing requires regular training and dedication despite the promises of various touch-typing packages. If handwriting is a weakness for a pupil, whether that be because of writing speed or legibility, then word-processing work can be transforming for them; even general familiarity with the keyboard is helpful.

The use of a word processor is a Joint Council Qualifications (JCQ) approved exam access arrangement and is commonly used by pupils who have difficulty with writing.

Resources that support all of the 'core deficits'

The resources listed `previously have been specifically described to support SEND pupils with 'core deficits'. Many form part of a 'low-tech tool kit' that is helpful to have at hand when you are supporting pupils in the classroom. By having this kit regularly available, pupils can become familiar with the contents and ultimately be able to use the contents independently, building their self-awareness and providing a low-cost route to engagement and ownership of their own learning.

The content of this kit can vary but it might contain sticky notes, index cards, stickers, plastic sticky tabs, coloured highlighters and markers, a mini-whiteboard, a manipulative toy and pens or pencils.

How it can be used

The kit can offer all pupils an opportunity to personalise their learning experience and better manage their own needs.

It offers myriad multi-sensory opportunities to support working memory, phonological processing and processing time. Each item can be used to manage learning more actively and appeals to a pupil requiring a higher level of sensory feedback. The kit should encourage a self-help approach encouraging pupils to develop their own personal strategies for effective learning.

The Low-Tech Tool Kit

Using general visual cues from walls, washing lines and tables

Classroom displays can provide essential visual cues that can be used to support working memory, recalling sequences, developing sight vocabulary and embedding a culture of self-help. These don't necessarily need to be ornate, permanent or time-consuming endeavours.

It may be that classroom displays change in nature and purpose regularly. The first step in understanding and enhancing the impact of classroom displays is to audit the existing environment and investigate how useful it is to pupils in supporting their learning.

Display audit

In reference to a specific room in which TAs support a pupil, the TA can complete the checklist of the display items available and, either reflect independently, or discuss with their pupils, to discover more about the pupil's awareness and use of these features.

In the comment box, it might be useful to think of some of the **DR KEEPIT** agenda when considering the display and the purpose it serves.

Table 5.2 Classroom Display Audit

What is on wall/tables/ washing lines	Do pupils use this?	How does it help? DR KEEPIT
Number line		
Scaffold		
Key words on walls		
Grammar charts		
Phonic grids		
Pupils' work		
Posters		

Table 5.3 Resources Inventory

Resource	Human	Material	Technological	Therapeutic
Working memory				
Phonological processing				
Slow speed of processing				
Sensory needs				

Resources inventory

It might be useful to conduct an inventory of resources in your area (Table 5.3). The table can be used to support this task. The important thing is to have a clear idea of what materials, tools and digital resources are available and if additional time or training is needed to become proficient in their use. This might be especially relevant in reference to digital resources and schemes focused on a specific difficulty or area of the curriculum. It may be that colleagues, class teachers and indeed the SENCO are willing and able to share their knowledge and skills and open up new possibilities for TAs in using existing materials and programmes.

Promoting a Focus on Learning Objectives

Why should TAs emphasise key points?

When we work in a school day after day, it can become like a second home. It's easy to forget that school can seem an obscure and confusing place for some children. Each moment of the day is filled with new experiences, collected together in oddly named segments; academic and subject specific language may be entirely unfamiliar outside of school. How many children will be able to unpack the jargon we use to talk about the curriculum? Understanding what mathematics 'is' and 'doing' mathematics aren't the same thing. For many children, the link between classroom activities and real life remains confusing. Helping pupils to make sense of their experience, to understand the relevance of the curriculum and its value, seems a sensible link to make if we are to secure their interest and sustain their effort.

TAs can play an important role in helping children to understand what they are being asked to learn and why they are being asked to learn it. This is aided by the fact that very often a TA spends the better part of the school day in class with a group or an individual. They often have the opportunity to experience the curriculum alongside the children in a wide variety of settings and environments.

This gives TAs an opportunity to see how (and if) it connects.

Making links is an important part of learning. Finding and understanding connections between words, numbers, facts and ideas allows us to transfer what we learn at school into the rest of our experience. Making links in learning creates depth and breadth of knowledge; it creates those moments when the 'penny drops' and one piece of information slips into place, revealing the bigger picture. It's like that bit in *The Last Crusade* when Indiana Jones steps out across a chasm to find there is a stone bridge under his feet; a handful of sand reveals the path – sometimes we need a little help to see what's right in front of us.

This section focuses on why, and how, to be clear about the aims and learning objectives of the curriculum. To be able to support learning most effectively, we have to know and understand how the learning objectives of any lesson relate to the syllabus being taught, and indeed, to the curriculum offer as a whole. We need to know why this lesson is important and we need to be able to identify and support the teaching and learning of the key points within it.

Having identified these key points, they can be emphasised, reinforced and connected. This happens by a process of checking understanding, supporting focus and providing thinking time.

Emphasising key points to support the 'core deficits'

Working memory

Clearly a child who struggles with working memory requires a strategy to support efficient use of their processing capacity. This means ensuring that the task at hand is fully understood and the points of reference are available and clear.

It's important that the nature of the knowledge being shared, however abstract or sophisticated, should not be further obscured by complex processes or conventions.

Making resources available, uncomplicating logical instructions and making routines easy can be straightforward ways to support a learner who struggles with working memory. Key points for learning can get lost in irrelevant details, comments or corrections that distract from thinking and processing. TAs need to remember that poor working memory is not evidence of low intelligence or limited understanding; being clear about the key points of a lesson allows appropriate challenge to be retained and the focus to be on knowledge, skills and understanding, which preserves the working memory capacity.

> 'Poor working memory is not evidence of low intelligence or limited understanding.'

In the book *The Dyslexic Advantage* by Eide and Eide (2011), there is an interesting section on the disadvantage given to dyslexic learners by placing too much emphasis on small steps in learning, in the absence of presenting them with the 'big picture'. They suggest that pupils with a dyslexic profile – often pupils with poor working memory – have a number of compensatory strengths. They identify that dyslexics often benefit greatly from contextual information and get the 'gist' of learning whilst struggling with recall of details. They talk about 'top-down' pupils who suffer in classrooms where information is fed to pupils, piece by piece; 'without a big picture framework to hang their knowledge on, the information is simply incomprehensible' (Eide & Eide, 2011, p. 99).

Phonological processing

Access to key points can be seriously hampered by poor phonological processing. If a pupil fails to hear, process, understand and retain auditory information, they are likely to miss out on key information and instructions given verbally. They may need to be supported in a number of ways other than straightforward repetition.

Further, if a pupil's phonological processing problems have delayed their reading and spelling skills, it is going to be necessary to be very clear about the nature of the challenge being set for them. Identifying the key points may mean not emphasising other challenging aspects of the task. Without this consideration, every lesson has a tendency to focus on the barrier and not the knowledge. A history lesson becomes a reading fluency session; a science lesson is about setting out a page neatly; a food technology lesson becomes about spelling. Pupils with SEND face challenge in school, period! Every day, and every lesson, is full of language, literacy, numbers, symbols and sequences; much of this is assumed knowledge for other children of the same age. The TA and the teacher have an opportunity to decide what the pupil should be putting their efforts into at any time, the form of the response or its content. This may vary. A lesson may well be about spelling, grammar or setting out a page, but that should be explicit rather than assumed. Sometimes it is necessary to offer support that compensates for phonological processing problems and their impact, and TAs should be offering to read and scribe, or support alternative means of recording using IT, so that a pupil can focus all their attention on the key points for *that* lesson.

Slow speed of processing

Allowing a pupil time to think is always helpful, but also allowing them the time to come back to and review key points is helpful. Finding ways to structure review into the lesson, to look over past work and to consider once again the place of this learning in the sequence, can help to embed skills and understanding.

How can TAs can emphasise key points to support the 'core deficits'?

There are a number of ways to tackle this in the classroom. It can be helpful to address the bigger picture. One of the biggest hurdles faced by TAs can be a lack of subject knowledge. This can obviously be more pronounced in a secondary or a post-16 setting where TAs might work across a wide range of subjects and in every Keystage. This can be further hampered by a timetable that does not include attendance at key meetings, training or meetings with teachers on a one-to-one basis.

In primary settings there may be more opportunities to liaise, due to greater contact with a smaller group of staff. Either way, TAs can still feel at a distinct disadvantage in some lessons, finding themselves acting reactively rather than proactively in terms of planning. This appears to be borne out across phases. Every time we lead TA training, one thing always comes up, and that's the need for *more time* to talk to staff about planning and co-ordination.

Creating time for regular liaison may be possible in some settings, but while we hope for an increase in resources, and therefore more time to think, breathe and plan a consistent approach to preparation, a clear set of expectations for the in-class role would certainly help. A good start is to seek out the big picture and refer to your school's documentation.

There will be a curriculum plan that maps all of the teaching and learning planned for a given period, across a range of subjects, and in terms of the pastoral and extra-curricular offer. From it, teachers will create programmes of study (POS) and schemes of work (SOW) that sequence and detail the activities. Sometimes (not always) there might be individual lesson plans that further detail specific Learning Objectives (LOs) and activities.

Programmes of study (POS): outline the plan for a period of time – usually without going into enormous detail.

Schemes of work (SOW): set out the content and often the activities for a shorter period – often a half term at a time. More detailed planning.

Whilst it would be unusual, and somewhat unfair, to expect a TA to spend their own time researching these documents in detail, it is vital that the lesson make sense to all professionals involved in its delivery. Without some notion of the bigger picture, it's very difficult to guide pupils to the key points in each lesson. The TA can help the pupil enormously by linking the big picture to the little picture.

It's helpful to:

- Have a POS or SOW for the lessons in which you support your students;
- Note what came 'before' and what comes 'next' in the sequence of lessons;
- Read the Curriculum Policy;
- Use time with the teacher to find out, and possibly highlight, the most important features of the SOW.

Create a key vocabulary list

Vocabulary is a cornerstone of school-based learning. Without recognising and understanding the meanings of thousands of words, it's impossible to unlock the curriculum independently. It is true that there are technological devices that can read, spell and even write for a pupil; however, constructing a relevant, meaningful sentence requires an understanding of the systems of language (its grammar) and an established and growing vocabulary.

How vocabulary is introduced and how it is to be remembered, used and embedded is a relevant question for all TAs and teachers, across all phases. A 'belt and braces' approach assumes that vocabulary should *not* be in place without explicit attention. New words (and words that pupils commonly misuse) should be introduced and explained, using both visual and auditory means. The words should be recorded and any contextual changes to meaning pointed out. When introducing new vocabulary:

- Be selective and explicit when introducing new words;
- Break down words into syllables in verbal and visual presentation;
- Explain where the word comes from;
- Explore and explain how it is linked to this and other subjects;
- Can it be visually represented – pictogram?
- Are common prefixes and suffixes helpful to explore?
- Use the word often and consistently – both say and show;
- Offer all of these listed tactics repeatedly – come back to new words;
- Reward pupil's use of the word in correct context.

Remember: those who struggle most in this respect may be those who are least able to express it.

Refine or adapt tasks

Children with SEND may take much longer to read text and to write independently than their peers. A well-crafted paragraph may take many redrafts; the conventions of a handwritten response are so laborious that they often constrain thought and limit memory, rather than give it structure. Simply teaching a pupil to touch-type and or to dictate using voice recognition software can be transformative, producing legible writing on the screen that can be manipulated and re-presented as necessary, and addresses many auditory and working memory issues.

TAs can help to create a varied range of possibilities for pupils to show their knowledge and understanding. Pupils with SEND may well require an alternative to the more conventional means of working, due to problems with literacy resulting from any of the underlying core deficits. It may be possible for a pupil to show their knowledge and understanding in a way that avoids the barriers to learning or at least minimises them. It's worth considering that instead of a written paragraph it might be possible for pupils to make an oral, visual, digital, multi-media or other response that utilises a strength or a skill.

Unless the task is specifically about proficiency in reading and writing, building in choice, in terms of outcome, can help the pupil to develop strategies to cope with the classroom and life outside school.

Review work

It's surprising how little time is taken looking back over what has been learned. In the case of pupils receiving support, it may be that there is little complete work at which to look. We have lost count of the 'book looks' we have conducted, where we cannot see the thread of progress, turning over blank pages, piecing together LOs and pupils' work, like stitching fragments into a quilt.

When we work with adults in training settings it's unusual not to share printed information, identify key learning points and the sequence of session before we begin, and children with SEND would also benefit from these principles. In situations where literacy is delayed and recording information is laborious, key points need to be provided and recorded by TAs and teachers.

For pupils with relevant work in their books and folders, returning to the previous lesson's work is a useful place to begin in checking understanding, making links and embedding the key vocabulary.

Offer a summary

It might be possible to bring together, in brief, a complete summary of the material that has been covered in a lesson. Summarising is a skill that we often work on with pupils to develop but it can have real usefulness in supporting pupils who struggle with auditory memory. To recall and recap the content of a class discussion, or question and answer session, setting out not only the end point but revisiting the stages on that journey provides a useful opportunity to think through and revisit the experience and the sequence of events. By using summary in this way to recap and rehearse a class discussion, the teachers can help to support working memory and refer to the bigger picture context.

Refer to visual cues in the classroom

Most classrooms have a plethora of information around the walls. This is discussed in more detail in the section on **Resources** (page 59). It's likely that key points for learning are available to reference. It may be that pupils need to have these pointed out and positioned in such a way to see, use and potentially contribute to them.

Check understanding

If we identify key points, context, introduce and embed vocabulary, help a child to find and use resources and adapt tasks to focus on the learning objectives, we are already going some way to build knowledge and understanding. 'Checking in' with pupils about all of this is a key task for the TA.

'Checking in' works on a variety of levels; there is the 'checking in' that happens when a child fails to follow a single instruction and the omission or delay is obvious; there is the 'checking in' during a task at hand, that the materials and steps are accessible for them; and there is the 'checking in' that happens after the event about what they have learnt, what they remember and how it has changed what they know and what they can do.

However, academic progress is rarely instantaneous, and understanding isn't necessarily immediate. It's not always realistic to expect measurable strides forward in every lesson. There is sometimes an unspoken assumption that children should 'get it' at their first attempt. This creates pressure on everyone to learn at the same rate. We know that additional processing time is vital to children with SEND. The quickest response to a question isn't necessarily the best response. The speed of a pupil's response is sometimes incorrectly seen as a sign of success, intelligence and engagement.

TAs can 'check in' over a period of time and make space for pupils to think, allowing understanding to grow and develop. Encouraging pupils to reflect on their learning can provide an opportunity for them to demonstrate the same levels of understanding as their faster processing peers.

It might be necessary for the TA to alert the teacher to the need for a change in pace, or to create the necessary time to secure and consolidate key concepts. Securing the same learning objective might well require an adjustment to the task or a modified outcome.

> 'The speed of a pupil's response is sometimes incorrectly seen as a sign of success, intelligence and engagement.'

ENGAGEMENT

Focusing on Thinking

Why is pupil engagement important for TAs?

Supporting a pupil's engagement in lessons means supporting a way of working in which the pupil does the cognitive heavy lifting. When engaged in learning, they should pay attention and participate, but more than that, they should demonstrate intellectual curiosity. They should be flying manual and not switching to autopilot (getting you to do it!) at the first sign of turbulence.

TAs can work to embed practices that support attention, participation and intellectual curiosity. If a pupil can begin to notice their habits in respect to these three, they can develop strategies to better manage the increasing demands of the curriculum.

What do we mean by engagement?

TAs can look for evidence of engagement in **attention, participation** and **intellectual curiosity**.

Attention begins with actually being in the lesson. You can't attend something if you are elsewhere. Monitoring a pupil's attendance on given days and during lessons is rule number one for supporting engagement.

Participation is hard to judge other than by comparison between pupils with SEND and their non-SEND peers; is this pupil *doing* something, and is it the same thing as the other pupils are doing? TAs might notice if they are completing a task to the same standard and at the same rate as their peers, and whether or not they are taking an *active* role.

Intellectual curiosity is something that is not so clearly measured. Does the pupil show signs of interest in their learning? The problem here is that pupils may well be deeply curious about topics outside of the standard curriculum. From football to film-making, schools are often full of young experts who live and breathe some special interest. Looking at how we can bring that enthusiasm and curiosity into their schoolwork, is often essential for children with SEND.

Addressing engagement to support the 'core deficits'

Working memory

Clearly all of the features of engagement described previously are likely to be affected by a poor working memory. If a child is struggling to access the vital, parked information they require to engage in a task, they are likely to become frustrated, lose motivation, disengage and let their attention move on.

It's difficult to take part in a conversation about learning and get involved in the classroom discussion if you can't keep the content of that discussion (the questions, answers and comments) in mind, no matter how deeply you are thinking, or how original the thoughts.

Phonological processing

Pupils with phonological processing difficulties experience a lack of easy access to the written word. When reading or writing independently, this means that often attention and engagement is functioning at word level, rather than at a sentence level. Thinking about a sentence as a piece of sense, it follows that whilst a child is struggling to make sense of the individual letter shapes in front of them, or to transcribe the sounds they hear into words on the page, it's unlikely that there is capacity left for meaning and understanding.

Processing time

The longer it takes to process, often the less time there is to complete something, and even perhaps to do something genuinely interesting. Children with SEND may be struggling to 'keep up' in the mainstream classroom not simply because of their processing difficulties but because in an attempt to alleviate the pressure, there is a temptation to keep things simple. They may not get onto the more interesting aspects of a subject because their learning difficulties delay access to them, to the extent that the class has moved on before they get to apply and demonstrate their knowledge.

How can TAs support engagement?

Having already broken engagement down into attention, participation and intellectual curiosity, it's necessary to go further to identify practices that support pupils in this respect.

Attention

When we ask for a pupil's attention in school, we are usually looking for them to listen more actively.

A TA can model active listening by doing the following.

Recognising attention

If you look around at an average staff meeting you will see any number of adults in 'the act' of paying attention. Some may be exhibiting all the signs traditionally associated, described earlier in this section; stillness, eye contact, etc. However, we are pretty sure that you will see at least as many not doing those things but instead shifting in their seats, doodling, folding paper, chewing, tapping, drinking, fiddling with hair or clothing or picking at the surface and objects to hand. Adults have a wide variety of options available to accommodate their sensory needs, while they attend to language and process its meaning. It isn't a sign of disrespect to fidget and we've yet to hear a Head Teacher shout at a teacher to 'put that down' when they reach for a pen, or a Kit-Kat! Indeed, many of us knit, sew, iron or attend to other mechanical tasks while we watch a film or TV show. Our physical activities aren't a very good indicator of attention.

'Our physical activities aren't a very good indicator of attention.'

Experimenting with the use of doodling, manipulatives, chew toys, wobble cushions and fidget devices can all be extremely useful in soothing and supporting the attention of children with concentration difficulties, by addressing their sensory needs.

Obviously, in this same staff meeting, there may be some staff using laptops or phones who may be genuinely disengaged from the meeting and instead, engaged in an email exchange or other absorbing activity. The difference is, in this case, the behaviour involves language. It's very difficult to engage two sources of information simultaneously; in the same way that it is very difficult to listen to two songs or watch two films at the same time.

TAs should note that if pupils are tuned into their voice, it is likely that they are tuned out to the voices of others, and this may include the teacher. It is important to be sensitive to this when talking to pupils and make it clear where their attention should be directed. A child may well miss out on key information and opportunities if they are focused on the TA at the wrong time.

Use empathy

It's important to have some understanding of how it might feel to be a pupil struggling with learning. Being actively engaged in ongoing training or CPD can be a useful tool to build this kind of empathy. Empathising with a pupil should be a prompt to offering considerate support, not a springboard to take on the challenges they face in their place.

Consider non-verbal behaviour

Some pupils with SEND will be watchful of and notice a great deal of our non-verbal behaviour. They may read our facial expressions and the way we respond to them. Other pupils, for example those with an autistic spectrum disorder (ASD), may struggle with this aspect of communication. Either way, it is important that TAs are aware of their habits and recognise these as non-verbal signals, explaining or modelling them as necessary. This includes the basics of conversational etiquette, eye contact, distance, etc. and where TAs are positioned in the classroom.

Offer a paraphrase

This is a device often used in coaching conversations where the listener holds back on advice or opinions, and instead rephrases what they have heard and offers it back to the speaker. It can be a very useful tool for a TA as it gives everyone a chance to review and clarify what has been said. There are a number of 'scripted' ways to lead into a paraphrase. Try one of the following before working on your own versions:

- 'You seem to be saying . . .'
- 'If I've understood correctly . . .'
- 'Am I right in thinking . . .'

When the pupil has listened to your version, they can have the opportunity to correct you or add to what they have said, making their meaning clearer and revealing any misunderstandings. It can be a very helpful way to make sure that a pupil knows they have been listened to, building confidence and trust.

Ask a question

This is a key skill for TAs and teachers. However, it is an aspect of the classroom conversation that tends to be spontaneous and unrecorded – what works and what doesn't can be lost in the ether. It's also very unlikely that there is any kind of system in place to help TAs monitor, vary and develop their questioning techniques, or to reflect on the impact of the questions they might ask pupils with SEND.

TAs can play a really important role in questioning and in modelling how to ask useful questions for the pupils they support. Different kinds of questions create different kinds of opportunities for a response. The impact of a question entirely depends on what is asked, and indeed, how and when it is asked.

TAs can refer to all aspects of the **DR KEEPIT** agenda and develop questioning habits that facilitate useful conversations about learning; encouraging pupils to reflect on resources; review key points; stay cognitively engaged; keep motivated (encouragement); address issues of proximity; identify barriers; and chunk tasks. Specific and open questions about this agenda are more likely to elicit a useful response that more general enquires such as: 'How are you getting on?' or offers of help like: 'Is there anything I can do?'

For examples of open and closed questions see Resource One, page 110.

Participation

In its simplest terms, it's hard to participate in something if you aren't in the room or are separated from the experience in some way. There is a whole range of access issues to be addressed if pupils with SEND are to be afforded the best chance of full participation in lessons.

If children seem not to be participating in lessons, it is likely that they are struggling to access one of the following:

- the space in which the learning is taking place
- the written materials being used
- the language that is used
- support from the teacher delivering the lesson.

The reasons for that struggle may be because of their SEND or may be connected to their personal circumstances such as their health and well-being. Lack of participation manifests in a variety of forms, some passive and some active.

Looking for patterns of participation can be very useful. The audit in Table 5.4 can help to map a pupil's participation across the school day and the curriculum, and in turn, act as a prompt to address any problem areas.

If a child can be rated 1–4 for participation across a week, areas of no or low participation may be identified and investigated.

Intellectual curiosity

Pupils with learning difficulties and SEND, like their non-SEND peers, require tasks that ignite their intellectual curiosity and challenge them to explore a subject, rather than tasks which offer repeated public opportunities to showcase their deficits in the name of closing the skills gap. If inclusion is to have any meaning and purpose, inherent in anything we ask pupils to do, should be an invitation to engage cognitively with the subject and to participate in the thinking. Therefore, unless a task has been created specifically to address individual strengths or weaknesses, there is more to be gained from encouraging pupils to attempt the same tasks, but with encouragement and opportunities, to establish additional personal strategies they might need in order to reach the objective.

Table 5.4 Pupil Participation Audit

	Monday	Tuesday	Wednesday	Thursday	Friday
Before school					
Registration					
Assembly					
Lesson 1					
Lesson 2					
Lesson 3					
Lunch					
Play					
Lesson 4					
Lesson 5					
Home routine					
Clubs					
Pick up					

Watching a pupil with an SpLD desperately trying to work in the same way as their peers is rather like watching a cyclist pedal furiously up a hill in a low gear, while a competitor sails past, with far less effort, in a higher one. They both may get there in the end, but the child with the learning difficulty is so exhausted they look for a flat route for the rest of the day, and therefore, it is likely that their levels of participation and engagement will significantly drop. Variations to tasks should diversify the route into and through the challenge, rather than simply offering a longer or a shorter path to demonstrating their existing knowledge or skills. Instead of differentiating the number, style and sophistication of a question, we need to think more about how many ways it is possible to arrive at an answer and the variety of ways to present it. This involves disentangling the process from the desired outcome and identifying the essential elements and which of those are flexible. It helps to ensure that any learning objective has a clear aim and rationale behind it, one which recalls the bigger picture, rather than simply comprising a list of tasks to be completed.

Intellectual curiosity is not necessarily about working to satisfy assessment criteria but rather about helping pupils who may be struggling at school to realise that there is time and there are options; learning doesn't stop when we leave school or the classroom – learning is for life and some of our most valuable learning experiences are not measured or even measurable.

Having equally high expectations of all pupils, despite identified barriers to learning, is essential – finding the edge and working to develop these strategies is uncomfortable but the core of the task at hand for the pupil and the TA.

ENCOURAGEMENT

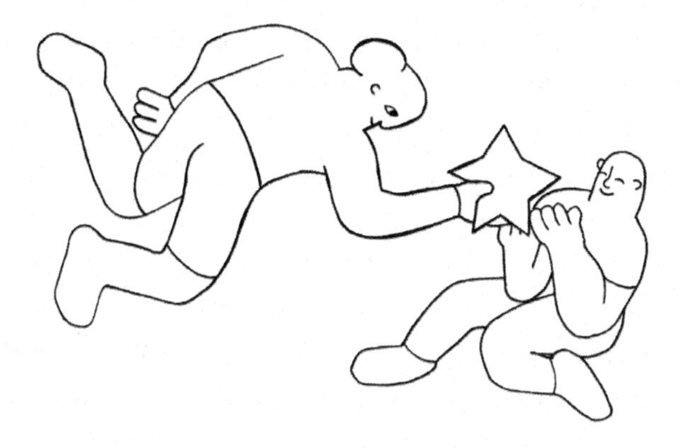

Promoting a Positive Attitude to School

Why is it important that TAs offer encouragement?

This section looks at how TAs can offer feedback to pupils about their progress in a way that develops self-awareness, confidence and sometimes the 'courage to fail'. Children with SEND are likely to be struggling to keep up with progress and attainment. Despite their best efforts, and very often due to delayed literacy, numeracy and processing speeds, school is a great deal more tiring for them than their peers. It's easy for them to become frustrated or discouraged and to lose motivation. Effective support is encouraging. It offers encouragement to try, and to keep trying; to attend and be attentive; to do the right thing and make good choices; and to acknowledge that success is possible. Finding a way to be supportive without being insincere, or removing the challenges from learning, is a very difficult task to balance. So how do we encourage children to persevere?

How do TAs encourage pupils to keep trying?

Assessment and Feedback – Most schools have detailed policies and established practices for assessment and marking. This is usually linked to a reporting schedule of written and verbal communication with parents. As we know, frequent feedback is a key part of the **MR CHUFI** agenda and central to teaching and learning.

When we offer a child our feedback on their work in school, we are taking part in an ongoing process of formative and summative assessment. This process is divided into two parts as it exists to do two things:

Summative assessment measures achievement, identifying the extent to which pupils can meet a set of criteria. Commonly, summative assessments tend to be referred to as 'tests' or 'examinations'. These measurements of achievement ultimately lead to qualifications. Qualifications acknowledge the knowledge and skills children acquired at school and give them a value; a currency with which greater opportunity is bought.

While TAs are sometimes involved in tests, exams and other aspects of summative assessment (including providing access arrangements), the feedback most often given by TAs is concerned with contributing to learning and helping a child to improve. TAs are more likely to be engaged in regular formative feedback.

Formative assessment should contribute to learning and is most often concerned with how a pupil might improve. Commonly, the formative assessment teachers offer pupils is referred to as 'marking'. Research done by the Education Endowment Fund in 2016 recommended that marking should be 'meaningful, manageable and motivating' (Independent Teacher Workload Review Group, 2016, p. 5)

How can a TA make sure the content of classroom feedback is 'motivating'?

It is helpful if the formative feedback that TAs offer to pupils conforms to these principles. The encouragement pupils receive from TAs can often be essential to building positive self-esteem. Unfortunately, in 2020 it's still likely that pupils with SEND have received more than their fair share of negative and confusing feedback as the system struggles to identify, to understand and ultimately to mitigate their difficulties. They may well have had experiences at school where they have been embarrassed or even humiliated as a result of their learning difficulties. This makes it extremely important that TAs (and teachers) carefully consider the impact of their feedback on motivation. When offering feedback, it's helpful for TAs to:

Link longer term aspirations to short term goals

In 2018 the Government published data showing that only 6% adults with learning disabilities were in paid employment (Measures from the Adult Social Care Outcomes Framework, 2018). Thinking about long term goals, further and higher education, training and careers is an essential task for those who support pupils with SEND. If the work we do in school in addressing barriers to learning fails to deliver in terms of future opportunities, our pupils are likely to face a challenging reality in their adult life.

The fact is, students who fail to develop sufficient skills in literacy, numeracy and social language, and who leave the system without qualifications, face an uncertain future. Securing and maintaining the motivation of pupils with learning difficulties is perhaps the biggest challenge of all. Meaningful and manageable systems of feedback have to take into account the need to encourage and motivate pupils and recognise the struggle of learning. Whilst it is important to recognise the small steps in learning, it is also important to know something about a child's aspirations and expectations for the future, whether that is focusing on transition to the next school, post-16 education, or training and employment. It is impossible to link long term goals to short term targets without clear knowledge of those future aspirations.

Know your baselines

It's crucial that we offer feedback with a clear understanding of the pupil's current level of ability and knowledge. If the specific areas of strength and weakness are overlooked, it's impossible to discern effectively if a pupil is progressing. Feedback that simply refers to age-related expectations can become punitive and demotivating. Children who are not yet achieving age-related expectations may still be achieving and progressing in relation to more individual targets. Keeping abreast of the incremental achievements and small successes is an essential part of building confidence.

Acknowledge the impact of fatigue

Children with SEND often have to work much harder and for longer to achieve at a lower level than their peers. They are often exhausted by the school day. It's important to recognise and acknowledge effort and tiredness. UK school hours are some of the longest in Europe.[1] Unfortunately, the impact of 'core deficits' can be greater the more tired pupils become. Having some awareness of this and offering pupils some support in the form of movement breaks, hydration, or a brief change in task can help to alleviate the problem.

Acknowledge setbacks and failure

Some classrooms now have displays that celebrate the learning journey and recognise the mistakes inherent in the first attempts at something new. They illustrate errors and reveal the opportunities they offer. This kind of accepting approach can be more difficult to manage in oral communication. When talking to a pupil about a misunderstanding or error, it's important to be accurate and clear to avoid further confusion. Some examples are:

- 'I think you might need to check the instructions again.'
- 'It might be helpful to refer to . . .'
- 'I can see why you might think that, but . . .'
- 'Can we try it this way?'
- 'I'm not sure that will work.'
- 'Let's work through an example together.'

Many TAs will be working in schools that have adopted the Mindset approach set out by the psychologist, author and TED talker Carol Dweck. In her book *Mindset* (Dweck, 2017), she explores the benefits of making an explicit link between effort and outcome in our feedback to pupils, encouraging teachers to be realistic and clear. At times when children fail to meet an expectation, she suggests the teacher add 'not yet' to their feedback; this balances reality and optimism. If TAs were to adopt Dweck's method, feedback should focus on the strengths in the learning process (activity/effort/application), rather than congratulate pupils for their personal talents and qualities.

Some examples of this approach are:

- 'You have understood this process very well.'
- 'I am impressed by your concentration with this task.'
- 'This section is written well. I can see that you have attempted to use some new vocabulary.'
- 'Your listening skills are improving. You have recognised all the key information.'

Maintain high aspirations

Easy to say, hard to do! Managing expectations for pupils with SEND is complicated. In order to set and maintain a high level of expectation, it's necessary to assume that with the right support, *all* pupils could achieve at a higher level than they could without support. In general, teachers and TAs want to personally make a positive difference to pupils' levels of achievement and well-being. In doing this and maintaining these high aspirations, we communicate to pupils with SEND that they should enjoy the same choices as all school leavers; to progress to further education and beyond to higher education, or a vocational course, apprenticeship, training for a fulfilling career and greater independence. This positive attitude can be expressed in a TA's actions, words and body language.

Maintain challenge and minimise pupil stress

Issues of compliance, equipment and procedure can dog pupils with SEND and SpLDs. Promotion of a *'high challenge, low stress'* environment can be done in any setting. We have previously mentioned the importance of making rules and routines logical and easy to follow. Making spare equipment available and responding to disorganisation with pragmatism and as calmly as possible means that energy is saved for intellectual effort and not excuses and conflict. Routine and consistency should replace fussy formality. It should be straightforward to make it as easy as possible for the pupil to do the right thing, to be in the right place at the right time with the right equipment and the right attitude.

Be kind

The messages we send to pupils about the value of their work have lasting impact. Kindness goes a long way and can make it less likely that pupils have an uncomfortable time in the classroom. It's easy to forget how self-conscious young people often feel, especially if their behaviour in response to this is defensive or dismissive. Thankfully, most of us can remember someone who was kind to us at school. It's difficult to define what this consists of but it seems easier to recognise when we see it or feel it. We know that children often judge themselves simply and harshly in comparison with others. Pupils with SEND may feel extremely sensitive about their difficulties and ignore their strengths. The feedback we give, and the way we deliver it, is a powerful opportunity to challenge or reinforce a pupil's belief about themselves.

How can a TA make sure the content of feedback is 'meaningful'?

Meaningful, formative feedback is specific. It enables the pupil to progress. It has to be accurate and it has to create options. The pupil needs to be able to understand and to *use* the feedback. Supporting a pupil in adopting a metacognitive approach to learning may be more helpful than offering feedback about degrees of success or failure.

> **Metacognition**: awareness and analysis of one's own learning process.

Feedback which supports metacognition is geared to enhance self-awareness, encouraging a pupil to observe and evaluate the way they have been learning. Some examples are:

- 'It's great to see you planning using the white board.'
- 'Well done, for remembering the right equipment.'
- 'That's a useful question.'
- 'I'm really glad to see you trying so hard to find the error in this . . .'
- 'It was good to see you working independently today.'
- 'You made some great connections today.'
- 'Looking back in your book to find the information was the right thing to do.'
- 'I was really happy to see you helping yourself by using the equipment in the tray for maths today.'

How can a TA make the content of feedback 'manageable'?

There are lots of opportunities for *oral* feedback. The good things about it are that it is usually immediate, in context, frequent and allows for questions. The less helpful things are that it can be difficult to process, remember and act on, if it isn't recorded in some way. The fact that it tends to take place in the public environment of the classroom can be embarrassing for pupils if things aren't going well. Also, there is always the possibility that there could be a mixed message from the teacher and TA in the feedback that the pupil receives.

Some TAs are invited to offer *written* feedback, which provides an opportunity to record progress and interactions so they can be returned to later. However, the success of this approach depends on legibility of writing, a pupil's reading skills and the TA's opportunity to check whether the pupil has understood. Lots of written feedback can also be somewhat alarming and overwhelming, whatever its content and intention.

Solutions for TAs to deliver effective feedback

There are a number of easy to use, low-tech and high-tech options for taking the best of oral and written feedback and making it more manageable for pupils with SEND. This can help address gaps, omissions and corrections and can prompt recall whilst promoting self-esteem.

TAs might like to use:

Removable tabs and sticky notes

Unlike marking in pen and putting comments in a planner, sticky notes are temporary and can be removed, keeping the work 'clean'. They can also be used by TAs and pupils to do a number of helpful things: indicate errors or successes, highlight the metacognitive processes of learning, flag difficulties as they arise, indicate there is a question to ask, highlight spelling, offer a suggestion or indicate a teacher's marking.

These methods are almost universally applicable in every subject, offering the opportunity to create communication that supports memory via simple colour codes or symbols, dates and annotation.

These semi-permanent feedback tools have the additional advantage of facilitating an ongoing conversation with the pupil, which can include the teacher, therapeutic specialists or parents, without additional administrative difficulty or replication.

High-tech solutions

Using a laptop or a tablet to complete work and to interact with staff using tools such as Google Educator or Microsoft Innovative Educator. To work effectively, a number of practical hurdles must first be overcome:

- ✓ consistent access to a working machine (linked to the necessary networks, printers, wi-fi);
- ✓ wi-fi and technology access at school and home;
- ✓ pupil cooperation – being seen as different might result in reluctance or refusal to use available technology;
- ✓ training and confidence levels of pupils and staff.

In the current climate, the Spring 2020 lockdown, the use of remote learning platforms have proliferated and this last bullet point has been addressed to a large extent in teacher populations – it remains to be seen whether schools have been able to train and to utilise TAs in the process of online learning.

What is a TA's role during tests and examinations?

The TA is often the professional who sees, first hand, the impact of testing and examinations for pupils with learning difficulties. TAs often provide support with preparation and revision, invigilating and providing access arrangements. Offering emotional support with children feeling the pressure at such times is often another aspect of this role. Clearly, the most important thing to do is to make sure TAs attend the invigilation training offered by the school and read any documents about their specific role during the test or exam.

What is a TA's role regarding diagnostic specialist assessments?

TAs may well be trained to administer a variety of one-to-one, non-specialist diagnostic assessments, possibly testing reading comprehension, phonological knowledge, spelling, numeracy or handwriting. Pupils may then go through a process of more in-depth assessment with professionals in school and other relevant external agencies like educational psychologists or speech and language therapists. One-to-one assessments conducted by external therapists often form part of identifying the specific learning difficulties and educational needs of a pupil. This can cause both disruption and great anxiety for pupils, and for their families, too. The TA might find themselves collecting pupils to attend assessments, helping to prepare them beforehand or spending time talking through the experience afterwards.

The SENCO will have had to consult the pupil and parents to make these arrangements as they are required to give their permission for the assessment, which will often take place in a private space in school. If the process is part of a formal needs assessment, parents have the right to be present. The timing of these assessments is obviously dependent on the availability of the professional, but this may mean that a pupil is withdrawn from class, and minimising the disruptions that might make this too public is a good idea and can often be simply managed. The pupils may also need time after the assessment to process and recover from this unusual and often tiring experience.

When the report becomes available it is likely to be a substantial piece of work – an opportunity to understand its contents by talking to the SENCO or the specialist is helpful but clearly requires a degree of sensitivity and respect for the confidentiality of the contents.

How can TAs help pupils to manage their anxiety?

It is significant for TAs to recognise the disabling effects of anxiety and acknowledge just how difficult it might be for a pupil to express the need for help. While anxiety can show itself in all kinds of ways (nail-biting, poor sleep and tearfulness to name but a few), it's not always obvious and may result in withdrawal, avoidance or refusal to participate.

The 'emotion coaching' approach has done much to bring neuroscience into our understanding of pupil behaviour at school. Most of us are now familiar with the notion that in order to focus on learning, pupils need to be free of the unpleasant effects of adrenalin released at times of stress which triggers the 'fight or flight' response controlled by the sympathetic nervous system. In his book *Dyslexia and Mental Health*, Alexander-Passe looks at the knock-on effects of repeated stressful situations on pupils with the SpLDs (Alexander-Passe, 2015). The more stress and anxiety pupils feel in a specific situation, the more likely they are to anticipate these emotions when contemplating similar situations in the future.

The things that TAs can do to support pupils in managing their anxiety during examinations are mainly to do with accuracy, preparation and good systems for sharing information. Such things might include:

- Making sure that pupils know in advance about assessment and what exactly is being tested.
- Allowing pupils to become familiar with the room and its features, desk spacing, clock, etc.
- Explaining how long the test will take and how long they will stay in the room.
- Making sure rules for communication are explicit – asking questions, going to the loo, talking to peers.
- Having a 'practice run' so that pupils can get used to the format of the process and the paper.
- Offering advice about what to do if pupils get overwhelmed, upset, stuck or finish early. Have stress balls or sensory toys and spare equipment available.

It is likely that teachers will have taken the pupils through the format and rubric of any formal test, but TAs also need to be familiar with this if they are to be present in the room or offering access arrangements, especially in reference to instructions and rubric, blank pages and how to fill in answers and where they need to be written.

Sharing results of a specialist report

These detailed reports are confidential and can be highly sensitive documents including personal details, family and/or medical histories. General Data Protection Regulation (GDPR) means the storage and access to them has to be restricted and managed with care. Obviously, they should not ever be left in public view, either on open screens or on desks. However, the description of needs, information and recommendations regarding adapting the curriculum, planning and making provision is essential to those working with the pupil, meaning that some thoughtful sharing is necessary.

Comparing results

Children commonly compare their performances after tests, reducing the information to a simple hierarchy in class. This can leave children with SEND vulnerable. However, it is possible to be considerate and to avoid practices which might add to a child's concerns. Results can be shared in a variety of ways that minimise this experience. They can be shared individually, in small groups or at different times of the day, week or term, and can often be part of a wider discussion designed to celebrate successes and plan new goals.

Promoting Independence

Why should TAs consider proximity?

This section explores the issue of place; we look at where pupils and TAs physically find themselves in relation to each other, to teachers and the classroom environment. In considering these issues, we look for opportunities for children to become increasingly independent in their learning and their social interactions.

TAs are deployed in a variety of ways to support pupils with SEND:

- ✓ in support of a single whole class group, working with identified pupils;
- ✓ providing one-to-one support for a single pupil;
- ✓ working with a number of identified pupils across subjects and year groups.

TAs tend to spend the majority of their time in class or working on specific programmes with small groups. The expectation is that they work flexibly and follow the child, unlike teachers, who are generally based in a designated space where the children come to them. The deployment of TAs often changes regularly from term to term, year to year, or week to week.

Due to this mode of deployment, TAs are often without a specific base. Most don't have a desk, or sometimes even a locker, but share with colleagues in the staffroom or other staff common areas.

The physical space TAs most often inhabit is the classroom. Rarely leading the group from the front, the TA is usually located somewhere amongst pupils or around the periphery of the room. It's likely that while inclusive schools might look at ways to minimise support, which takes children out of the mainstream classroom, TAs often lead 'interventions' in shared, open 'break-out' spaces or a learning support area.

School life can engender a rather territorial approach to space delineated by clear boundaries. Teachers in all phases often have a classroom or group of rooms in which they teach regularly; some have separate workspaces or offices. When preparing or doing administration, TAs tend to inhabit space that 'belongs' to other staff.

Could it be that it is this absence of a designated physical space that ties TAs and pupils so tightly and often so unhelpfully together? In the absence of an established place to work both in the classroom and in the staffroom, TAs become almost tethered to pupils. In order to be effective in supporting pupils, TAs need a place to be and a clearly defined role in the school. Unfortunately, TAs often literally don't know where they stand, or sit!

Proximity that supports 'core deficits'

When TAs are in a fixed position, sitting constantly adjacent to the pupils they support, any one or all of the following may happen:

- ⊘ Pupil can develop a 'learned helplessness', becoming overly reliant on TAs to interpret lessons for them.
- ⊘ Pupils develop stymied social skills and peer relationships may suffer.
- ⊘ Teachers can become dependent on TAs to manage learning for pupils with SEND and take a back seat in adapting their own teaching and understanding of pupil needs.
- ⊘ TAs intervene too much or too quickly, in a well-meaning attempt to protect pupils from the failure.
- ⊘ TAs can become a barrier to academic development as they take on too much of the cognitive load.

Obviously, some pupils with SEND require close proximity and a high level of vigilance. However, this is less prevalent than the current model of in-class support would suggest. Ultimately, all pupils are entitled to as high a level of independence as their ability can support.

This requires teachers to work to adapt their teaching and supply an accessible task and useful resources. If this is in place, TAs can work to support the pupil in producing an outcome as independently as possible. TAs are there to support and 'check-in', not to oversee learning.

Instead of thinking about where a TA should be, they firstly need to consider what we would like to see the pupil doing and work back from there.

It's helpful to think about the following:

Pupil position

You may have the perfect opportunity to observe whether the pupil is best served by proximity to:

- ✓ source material
- ✓ the front of the classroom
- ✓ the teacher
- ✓ a specific piece of technology
- ✓ light or sound
- ✓ a peer
- ✓ a group of peers
- ✓ doors
- ✓ a TA.

Vigilance

If TAs sit adjacent to a pupil, it's also likely that they are overseeing their output quite closely. Whilst there may be circumstances in which this might be necessary, such as when a child is cutting or working with equipment, it is useful to consider how we ourselves would respond to such oversight when trying something new. In training TAs, a helpful exercise allows them to work under the close eye of a colleague and then repeat the exercise with a colleague standing by to help. It's not surprising that we all feel more self-conscious and embarrassed about our errors, and even our process, when we are being watched. It is even hard to type with someone at our shoulder! Being vigilant can be achieved from a short or even a long distance. This may well require an agreed system of communication and, perhaps, some rules for its use, but it frees the child to work uninhibited. They could signal for support from the TA with the movement of a pencil case, a coloured sticky note, or an object placed on the desk, or it may be 'hand-up'.

Grouping

It's important that our routines for checking proximity incorporate a degree of flexibility. A situation where a child's learning difficulty confines them to sit in the same seat, or with the same person, for the duration of their learning experience singles them out as different and is to be avoided. Exploring variations and encouraging paired, small group and whole class participation is vital.

If a child is to be included in the mainstream learning experience, a social experience of learning with other pupils forms an important part of that. As we know from the recent Timpson Review (2019), pupils with SEND spend a disproportionate amount of their time in isolation following incidences of poor and uncooperative behaviour. A huge number are permanently excluded. 'It is well documented that there are longstanding trends that children with SEN are more likely to be excluded, both for a fixed period and permanently, than those who do not have SEN' (Timpson Review, 2019, p. 36).

This suggests that children with SEND are not developing the social skills they need to cope in group situations. As a TA, supporting this skillset is a vital aspect of in-class support. Social skills are not a side issue; children who fail to develop these skills find themselves on the periphery of society and opportunity. To support the social aspect of learning, TAs can:

- Facilitate pupil-to-pupil contact
- Offer suggestions for conversation starters
- Model eye contact, distance and listening (see **Engagement**, page 78)
- Only sit with pupils when necessary.

Why should TAs identify barriers to learning?

The most important task for TAs is to support or help children with their work. With a vast number of TAs, this comes from a genuine place of care and nurture and this is usually the main reason why TAs embark upon this role.

The Education Endowment Foundation's report *Making Best Use of Teaching Assistants* discovered in their research that TAs often fail to 'encourage pupils to think for themselves' (EFF, 2015, p. 17). TAs have often been accused of *doing* the work for pupils as it seems to be a natural instinct to 'jump in' and to solve a problem when a child is struggling. It takes a great deal of self-awareness and self-control to notice a problem and then to step back, and attempt to identify the barrier the pupil is facing rather than immediately 'jumping in' and removing the barrier completely. For example: reading an entire text when a child is struggling; pointing out the answers for a comprehension; or measuring the angles in a geometry lesson. If TAs jump in and completely remove the barrier, the child is unlikely to remain cognitively engaged and this will not support their processing difficulties. The TA is there to facilitate the learning process, not to model it without adaptations.

IDENTIFYING BARRIERS

Recognising Barriers to Learning

Chapter 7, on The Needs Matrix, carefully explains when and how to use this comprehensive tool when considering a child's classroom behaviour and the specific barriers to learning they experience. As core deficits underlie so many difficulties in the classroom, similar barriers are likely to appear across all subjects of the curriculum and indeed in extra-curricular and unstructured time. The Needs Matrix offers TAs a detailed set of prompts to use for their observations of pupils; using it creates consistency in recording and monitoring a child's needs as they present themselves in different situations and over time.

The importance of questioning to identify and remove barriers to learning

We have already discussed the importance of using open and closed questions to cognitively engage, make links, check understanding and offer encouraging feedback. In identifying barriers, TAs need to be able to ask questions that elicit a useful and specific response from pupils, so that they can understand the stage that they are at in their learning and what is preventing them from moving forward.

The purpose of the TA's question should open up the learning conversation and prompt a pupil to engage, use the resources and think about their work.

Bloom's Taxonomy

In 1956, Benjamin Bloom devised a hierarchical ordering of cognitive skills that still helps teachers and educationalists to understand the stages of cognitive development that a child moves through in their learning. According to Bloom's Taxonomy, there are six stages of thought processing that move from lower to higher level thinking. All pupils, including those with SEND, can engage in higher level thinking. With some understanding of these levels, a TA can support a pupil in moving through them, often by asking the right questions or offering simple prompts.

The following table provides the six stages of Bloom's Taxonomy and suggests some prompt questions that can be asked to secure each stage and encourage the pupil to proceed to the next level.

Bloom's Taxonomy

Bloom's Taxonomy	Sample Questions for a TA to Use	Is Pupil Able To . . . ?
Stage 1: KNOWLEDGE (lower level thinking)	Can you . . . arrange, describe, duplicate, list identify, name, recognise, reproduce	Recall information and memorise facts
Stage 2: COMPREHENSION (lower level thinking)	Can you . . . describe, explain, summarise, estimate, discuss, give examples of, predict	Understand the meaning
Stage 3: APPLICATION (lower level thinking)	Can you . . . apply, demonstrate, produce, choose, change, show, solve, use	Apply their knowledge to a new situation or example
Stage 4: **ANALYSIS** (**higher level thinking**)	Can you . . . analyse, contrast, compare, organise, deconstruct, rewrite, formulate	Break down the information in front of them and analyse the importance of it
Stage 5: **SYNTHESIS** (**higher level thinking**)	Can you . . . reorganise, develop, combine, judge, conclude	Decide on how to proceed by looking at the evidence in front of them
Stage 6: **EVALUATION** (**higher level thinking**)	Can you . . . argue, appraise, evaluate, interpret, justify, construct, produce	Use existing knowledge and understanding and create a new example

By using the sample questions from Bloom's Taxonomy, a TA can ensure a pupil engages with learning at all levels, despite the barriers they face. Higher level thinking isn't only for those with higher level attainment. For example, a pupil may be stuck at Level 1 – knowledge – and be struggling to recall the facts when 'describing' or 'identifying' information. However, if a TA asks a Level 2 – comprehension – question, requiring them to explain or summarise, it may be possible to unlock their thinking and move them on whilst they are engaged. TAs might also discover that a pupil is further along in their understanding than they are able to demonstrate on paper, so this approach can be useful in offering adequate challenge to pupils with SEND.

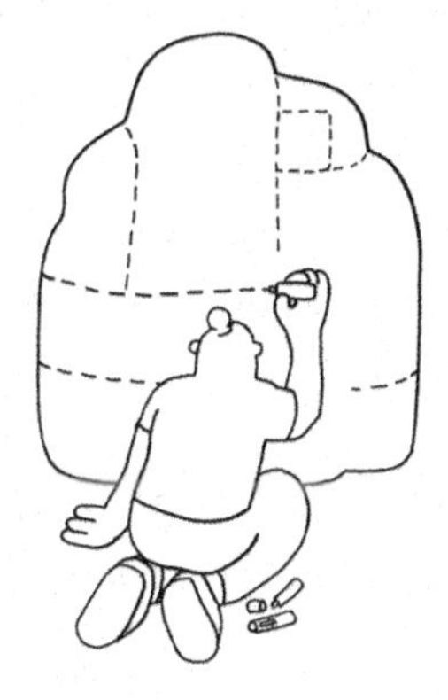

Adapting the Pace of Learning, 'Breaking it Down'

Why adapt the pace of teaching?

Pupils with SEND require access to the same learning objectives as their peers. In order to achieve these objectives, the tasks that illustrate them may need to be further broken down. Breaking tasks down into more manageable chunks can do the following:

- ✓ clarify the stages of a process
- ✓ articulate those stages
- ✓ create a sequence
- ✓ allocate appropriate time to a stage.

Sometimes adaptations to pace can result in pupils with SEND being offered a modified learning objective with a specific task calibrated to their level of ability, based on prior attainment. Instead of working on a common learning objective and chunking to identify the stages, concepts or processing within it, teachers or pupils may be tempted to create or to select a less challenging activity. Whilst at times this may be preferable, it is important to recognise that pupils with learning difficulties, particularly those with SpLD, are often underestimated when judged on average ability. Some sophisticated concepts may be readily understood and accessible if there is attention to supporting working memory and other core deficits. A simple scale of difficulty or more lengthy challenges may do more to limit than enable their attainment.

How TAs can use task chunking to support 'core deficits'

As we discussed in the previous section on identifying barriers, having regard to the load that a task might place on working memory, processing time and phonological skills acknowledges the specific nature of any challenge for individual pupils. Most classroom learning will present an additional challenge in some form for pupils with SEND.

Practical strategies for task chunking include:

- Instructions on a mini-white board;
- Numbered sticky notes on the desk or page;
- Highlighting a section of questions using a reading ruler;
- Working with a peer to break down the task and share it;
- TA distributing subtasks within group and facilitating co-operation;
- Using a timer to support awareness of the passage of time;
- Quick TA check-ins on completion of each stage;
- Offering rest/movement breaks between stages;
- Only sharing one requirement at a time;
- Estimating at the beginning how long each part should take and review while working;
- Setting mini-goals or targets and offering rewards or specific praise.

Managing time

Managing time is often a difficult task for pupils with SEND. They may struggle to estimate how much time a task might take them, and they may struggle to estimate or understand the time available. A TA can help a pupil to develop a sense of time, self-awareness and an ability to plan and prioritise by making this process explicit and breaking it down.

Prompting a child to notice the passage of time and use clocks and timers is a useful exercise for a TA.

Review and repetition

Pupils with learning difficulties often need to return, repeatedly, to concepts after explicit teaching is completed. Recall may not necessarily work predictably, and assuming steady and cumulative knowledge building is likely to result in disappointment and sometimes disagreement.

It is not uncommon for pupils with SpLDs to work with focus, to have shown their understanding and their ability to apply knowledge and then subsequently to struggle to repeat the process, particularly in a different context or while under duress.

Note

1 www.oecd.org/edu/EAG2014-Indicator%20D1%20(eng).pdf

Summary

What is the role for TAs in supporting differentiation and adaptive teaching?

- Pupils' learning difficulties are not necessarily specific to a single category of need as described in The Code. They are likely to have a unique combination of difficulties that occur to a greater or lesser extent across all four categories.
- Pupils' needs are likely to present differently across the curriculum, meaning they require support which responds flexibly and allows room for them to work independently and at different levels.
- The aim of differentiation and adaptive teaching are that all learners can access an appropriate education and enjoy the most effective teaching and learning experience.
- Differentiation is about noticing the differences between pupils as learners.
- Adapting teaching is about taking action to address differences so that they don't become disadvantages that reduce access and achievement.
- Children with learning difficulties are also children with learning abilities.
- Teachers can use the **DR GOPTA** acronym to differentiate and adapt teaching; they do this by considering Dialogue, Resources, Grouping, Outcome, Pace, Task and Assessment.
- The aim of this is to make the most effective learning opportunities available to all pupils so that they can Make Links, Take Risks, Engage Cognitively, Think at a Higher Level, Check Understanding, Share Feedback and Become More Independent (**MR CHUFI**).
- TAs already support the **DR GOPTA** agenda in a number of important ways.
- **DR KEEPIT** is an agenda we have devised specifically for TAs to ensure that task completion does not become more important than the other features of learning outlined in **MR CHUFI**.
- **DR KEEPIT** addresses Dialogue and Resources and to that adds considerations about Key Points, Engagement, Encouragement, Proximity, Identifying Barriers and Task Chunking.

Dialogue

- It's necessary for TAs to consider the purpose, content and form of their classroom talk.
- The conversation between the pupil and TA is a key part of a supportive classroom relationship. The TA is often in the middle of chain of communication between the teacher and the pupil.

- Using dialogue to support pupils with poor working memory requires a 'less is more' approach, as children may struggle to retain oral language.
- Poor speech sound processing further compounds difficulties with spoken language and so it is important not to speak too quickly or repeatedly re-phrase a message.
- The classroom talk tally invites an audit of existing habits for classroom talk.

Resources

- Supporting pupils with SEND requires material, human and technological resources.
- Every pupil has a unique combination of barriers to learning and therefore will benefit from a responsive and flexible approach to the use of these resources.
- Resources that support a child with poor working memory include mini-whiteboards, sticky notes and tabs and mind-mapping software.
- Resources that support a child with poor phonological processing skills include printed reference materials for spelling and vocabulary, reading rulers, highlighter pens, reading pens and computer readers.
- Resources that support pupils with slow speeds of processing include clocks and timers.
- A 'low-tech tool kit' is helpful in order to support all core deficits.
- Completing and sharing a resources inventory like the one on page 108 can be helpful in ensuring that the materials and equipment already available is familiar to all.
- A list of resources to support pupils with sensory processing difficulties can be found in Chapter 4.

Key points

- This section addresses the role of the TA in helping a pupil to make sense of their environment and the language and routines in which it is expressed.
- Making links is an important aspect of learning allowing what is discovered in the classroom to be applied to more than one subject and setting, linking school and the real world.
- The TA has an opportunity to help pupils understand how learning objectives fit into the broader curriculum and to highlight the key concepts on which future learning may be based.
- Pupils with poor working memory may lose out if tasks are broken down into too small or too complex a set of processes; keeping

the big picture in mind can help focus on the core learning objective.

- Pupils who struggle with reading and spelling are likely to miss out on lesson content if their literacy is not supported.
- Pupils with slow processing speed may benefit from regular opportunities to review prior learning and its context.
- TAs need access to curriculum planning in order to be clear about the order and priorities for any given period.
- Pre-teaching vocabulary is a helpful way to support all core deficits.
- Finding ways to adapt the outcome of a task and to play to a child's strengths can help focus on the key learning rather than the barrier.
- Reviewing and offering a summary can bring key concepts together.
- TA need a process for 'checking in' with a pupil to ensure they have understood concepts and expectations or if they need additional time or resources – this needs to take place over time and be an invitation for pupils to reflect on how they are doing.

Engagement

- Attendance has a significant impact on attainment.
- We look for attention, participation and intellectual curiosity as evidence of engagement.
- Pupils with poor working memory may be more likely to lose motivation and attention as they struggle to retain important information.
- Weak phonological processing may result in problems with reading and writing that prevent engagement with lesson content; as energy and focus is expended on managing the literacy aspect of tasks, opportunities for higher level thinking and processing are lost.
- If pupils are slow to process, they might miss the most important or most interesting aspects of a lesson as they struggle to keep pace with their peers.
- Supporting and modelling active listening can be a boost to attention. To do this it is necessary to be able to recognise attention in all its forms, use empathy, consider our non-verbal behaviour, offer paraphrases and develop a range of questioning techniques.
- Pupils with SEND may well have very different levels of participation across the curriculum. It can be useful to monitor this and observe and note the context of peaks and troughs. This can be done using Participation Audit.
- Linking learning to lived experiences and acknowledging the value of skills and talents outside the academic curriculum can do much to encourage intellectual curiosity and self-esteem.

Encouragement

- The focus in this section is how to share feedback in such a way as to develop self-awareness and confidence in the face of challenge.
- Formative and summative feedback shapes a pupil's understanding of their achievements and potential.
- TAs are likely to offer frequent formative feedback focusing on how a pupil might improve.
- Take steps to ensure that feedback offered in class is motivating.
- Manageable feedback is easy to understand, use and refer back to.
- TAs often offer pupils ad hoc oral feedback. While the content may be valuable and timely, it's difficult to retain.
- By using removal tables and sticky notes or review-type functions when word processing, this formative, on-the-spot feedback can be retained and used for reflection.
- TAs often have an operational role in formal assessments and examinations.
- Managing pupil anxiety can be an additional aspect of the TA role in this scenario. TAs can do much to support pupils with SEND in this respect. Refer to the list on page 91.
- Sharing information after tests and assessments requires careful consideration. Conversations about pupils may be necessary but the setting of conversations must be in private – not in a corridor, reception, classroom or other public space.

Proximity

- TAs work in a variety of spaces in school.
- It's important that pupils with SEND are afforded opportunities to work independently. TAs need a physical space to work in order to facilitate this.
- It's helpful to think about how a pupil's position in the room impacts their learning.
- Aiming for vigilance rather than oversight can create some space for a pupil to take risks with their learning.
- Looking at grouping and peer interaction is essential in developing social skills for learning.

Identifying barriers

- Facilitating learning requires a TA to help identify the barriers presented by a task and then support a pupil in finding ways to reduce them.
- Thinking about core deficits is a helpful way into this process.
- Asking useful questions is essential in identifying barriers. Becoming familiar with Bloom's Taxonomy can help structure and vary questioning. See page 97.

Task chunking

- Breaking a complex set of instructions into a simpler series of steps is a valuable skill to model for pupils with SEND.
- This 'chunking' can also support the pupil to develop better time management as they estimate how long a task may take and plan accordingly.
- Repetition and review can be built into the chunking process.
- Suggestions for managing task chunking can be found in the list on page 99.

Resources

Table 5.1 Classroom Talk Audit

Closed questions	
Open questions	
Instructions	
Praise words	
Pupils praised	
Reprimands	
Students sanctioned	
Checking understanding	
Pauses for thought	
Encouraging speech	
Grammar in speech	
Position when talking	
Repetition	
Managing misunderstanding	
Varying tone, volume and register	
Clarity of speech (staff)	
Pace of speech	

Table 5.2 Classroom Display Audit

What is on wall/tables/ washing lines	Do pupils use this?	How does it help? DR KEEPIT
Number line		
Scaffold		
Key words on walls		
Grammar charts		
Phonic grids		
Pupils' work		
Posters		

Table 5.3 Resources Inventory

Resource	Human	Material	Technological	Therapeutic
Working memory				
Phonological processing				
Slow speed of processing				
Sensory needs				

Table 5.4 Pupil Participation Audit

	Monday	Tuesday	Wednesday	Thursday	Friday
Before school					
Registration					
Assembly					
Lesson 1					
Lesson 2					
Lesson 3					
Lunch					
Play					
Lesson 4					
Lesson 5					
Home routine					
Clubs					
Pick up					

Open questions for each letter of ***DR KEEPIT***

Open questions to prompt effective **DIALOGUE:**

'What do you need to remember to complete this task?'
'What would you like me to do to help you start?'
'What would you like me to repeat to help you move on?'

Open questions to prompt effective use of **RESOURCES**:

'What resources might you need to complete this task?'
'Which resources do you have with you already and which do you need to go and find . . . ?'
'Are there any resources on the walls/displays that might help you . . . ?'
'Where might you find the resource that you need to help you complete this . . . ?'

Open questions to prompt effective **KEY POINTS**:

'What is this task asking you to do?'
'What are the stages you need to go through?'
'What can you remember about this topic?'

Open questions to prompt effective **ENGAGEMENT AND PARTICIPATION**:

'What might help you to listen?'
'What would help you to focus on the teacher?'
'Why do you think this is important?'
'Can you link any of these ideas to something you already know?'

Open questions to prompt effective **ENCOURAGEMENT**:

'What are you most proud of in this task?'
'What have you remembered from last time?'
'How could you improve your answer if you were to do the task again?'
'Explain to me how you completed this task so well.'

Open questions to prompt effective **PROXIMITY**:

'Where do you need sit so that you can be involved in the lesson?'
'Would you like me to sit or circulate so that I can support you in your work?'

Open questions to prompt effectively **IDENTIFYING BARRIERS TO LEARNING**:

'What part of the task this are you struggling with?'
'Point to the problem.'

Open questions to prompt effective **TASK CHUNKING**:

'How could you break this task up in smaller steps?'
'What are the most important parts of the task?'
'What do you think is the first step in completing this task?'

---

6 How can TAs contribute to the Graduated Approach for pupils with SEND?

In Chapter 1 we introduced the 'Graduated Approach'. This is set out in The Code as a structured whole-school approach to making provision for children with SEND and for those who are not progressing in line with age appropriate expectations. It's important to recognise that we may use this approach with children who are keeping up with expectations but appear to underachieve with aspects of learning in comparison to their peers. In order to make progress and benefit from education, children with SEND need an educational provision that is 'additional to or different from' the provision generally available to all (The Code, 2015). It's worth noting that the school policy on SEND or the SEND Information report (to be found on the school's website) should set out broadly what might happen within this Graduated Approach. Obviously, this is going to vary between phase and setting.

The SEND Information Report

The Code of Practice requires all schools to publish on their website a SEND Information Report which should include:

- the kinds of SEN that are provided for
- policies for identifying children and young people with SEN and assessing their needs, including the name and contact details of the SENCO (mainstream schools)
- arrangements for consulting parents of children with SEN and involving them in their child's education
- arrangements for consulting young people with SEN and involving them in their education
- arrangements for assessing and reviewing children and young people's progress towards outcomes. This should include the opportunities

available to work with parents and young people as part of this assessment and review
- arrangements for supporting children and young people in moving between phases of education and in preparing for adulthood. As young people prepare for adulthood outcomes should reflect their ambitions, which could include higher education, employment, independent living and participation in society
- the approach to teaching children and young people with SEN
- how adaptations are made to the curriculum and the learning environment of children and young people with SEN.

(The Code, 2015, 6.78)

This Graduated Approach makes up a cycle.

This system for school-wide response replaces those described in the previous Codes of Practice. It is new and different in that it is a cycle, not a hierarchy. Previous SEND systems looked much more like pyramids than circles; they described a linear process to help schools identify groups of vulnerable children. Those with the most severe or persistent needs would be prioritised. This often led to access to external agencies to investigate needs or led to a statutory assessment by the LA. This process was designed to both identify and describe the learning difficulties and the special educational needs arising from them, so that the school might allocate resources accordingly. These systems arranged pupils in stages 1–5 and named groups like 'school action' and 'school action plus'. However, the current cycle (The Code, 2015) is a stripped back rationale which provides a set of principles rather than a set of instructions in terms of identification and action.

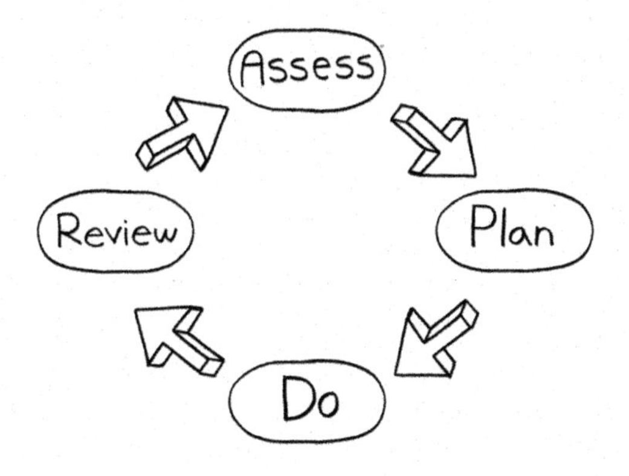

The cycle is supposed to ensure that having identified an initial concern, which may be evidence of a learning difficulty, that schools act on that assessment and offer something to address it. Having done so, there is then a review looking at how successful it has been. It is easy to trace this rationale through to the Education Inspection Framework mantra of 'Intention, Implementation, Impact' (EIF, 2019).

The most important aspect of a cycle is that one action leads directly to another, that the rationale makes sense, and the thinking is joined up. The work involved in assessing, planning, doing and reviewing has to be co-ordinated in such a way that teachers and TAs can cope with any additional or different demands placed upon their time.

How do TAs keep track of the Graduated Approach cycle?

It's likely that TAs have some overview of the SEND register and can see that some pupils are coded to indicate two categories; those with an EHCP in place or those receiving SEND support, meaning that the school is making provision for the child's SEND within its own resources. However, it is not likely to be clear from any pupil-specific data at which stage of the cycle a child might be. In fact, it's highly likely that pupils will be at different stages of this cycle at any one time. Some pupils will be in assessment, some in the midst of a planned intervention, others in review. SEND processes, including Annual Reviews and diagnostic testing, don't necessary align with school schedules and routines, but instead depend more often on the date that EHCPs are issued which occurs year-round. Also, the timing of a cycle may look different for each pupil depending on what we know about their needs and learning difficulties, their age and phase. For example, a recently identified child might be involved in a more sustained and detailed period of assessment which might involve many aspects from 'round robin' type feedback from teachers, to the recommendations of a specific diagnostic assessment, to their history of results from whole school assessments. A child new to a school or a class, with an existing EHCP, is going to be experiencing a rather different approach to assessment in that teachers are likely to be looking at their progress in relation to the outcomes identified on the EHCP, Individual Education Plan (IEP) or other individual planning.

Whilst TAs may not have the opportunity to set out the plan for this cycle, they no doubt contribute to it at every stage. It's entirely possible that a TA contributes to assessment, either by administering it or supporting the process in some way through access arrangements. It may be that teachers and SENCOs are keen to hear the TA's views in the planning stages; they may have particular knowledge relating to an individual, a specific area of need or indeed an intervention that may inform a new Plan. This can be where the voice of the TA is lost – without good systems for ongoing and clear recording, reporting cannot be well informed.

What happens at the end of a cycle is largely decided by the SENCO. It may be that a child goes through a number of cycles before a decision is made to seek an EHC needs assessment from the LA, or indeed, to consult an external specialist for more advice. The fact that this cycle can return to the beginning, and begin again, makes it more important than ever that we show vigilance in noticing the effect and impact on a child's needs. We have long been opponents of any system that waits for a child to fail, and to fail again, before adequate measures are taken to look more closely at their individual profile. It is not only weeks and months of progress and attainment that can slip away, but self-esteem, motivation and trust in us that ebbs away with it.

In the section that follows we are going to set out a number of approaches and formats for tracking the processes of the Graduated Approach so that, at any time, TAs can work with awareness of each stage of the cycle and offer useful feedback on the pupils they support, and their role in its provision. Our approach is designed to be quick and easy to use but to prompt a more specific record than traditional narrative record-keeping that tends to focus on alarms and excursions, rather than the daily business of learning.

1. Keeping track of 'Assess'

The only direction about 'Assess' provided in The Code is that schools should assess children's current skills and levels of attainment on entry, and regularly review progress to identify underachievement.

There are no specific instructions about the form, the focus or the frequency of the assessments to be completed in the 'Assess' stage of the cycle. In this cycle Assess serves to establish a base of evidence from which to start. A TA may be working with the class teacher to support children who are not meeting expectations in regard to their progress or attainment.

Underachievement implies that a child could be, and should be, achieving more than they are currently able to demonstrate. It might mean that they are not achieving in line with their peers or it might mean that they are not achieving in a way that is consistent with their own previous performance.

A robust and responsive assessment process should help to establish whether or not there is a learning difficulty, and an unmet special educational need preventing this level of achievement. Sustained concern about a child's progress and attainment may generate a range of assessment opportunities. The Assess stage may be about commissioning additional testing but it should also be about looking at the data already available, considering its use and validity in light of any concerns.

An overview of a child's performance across the curriculum is a key starting point. Again, it's essential to remember that children with learning difficulties are likely to perform at very different levels and at different rates in different subjects and settings.

Understanding baselines

One of the more unhelpful features of our current education system is the inconsistent language we use to describe the test results for basic skills. Sight reading, reading comprehension, mathematics and spelling skills are measured and reported on via a bewildering variety of technical assessment jargon. Each generation has had to familiarise itself with a new system of stages, levels, grades and numbers, each ascribed a value that should translate into something like sense. Essentially, everything is 'norm' referenced, in that we make judgements on individual ability based on how the majority of those tested perform at a certain age. Those who cannot reach or who exceed the performance of the majority will always be fewer and fewer in number the further their score is from the average.

Baseline scores might be in the form of the following:

An age, in years and months: the information provided identifies any difference between the child's chronological age and the score they will have received in a specific test, such as a test of reading or spelling.

A standardised score: the score is calculated in reference to an age-related national sample. A standardised score (SS) of 100 indicates an average performance in the test. SSs exist within numerical boundaries indicating low, well below and above, and well above average.

A raw score: a direct representation of the number of correct or incorrect responses in a specific test.

A percentile ranking: score with a percentile ranking of 1 indicates that 99% of the age-related sample would do better in the same test; the higher the percentile ranking, the better the performance.

Schools generally have a variety of baseline scores available for pupils across all Keystages; from the end of Keystage testing to standardised measures of cognitive ability which include verbal and non-verbal reasoning skills. The important thing when considering or using assessment data is to first be clear about what exactly is being measuring and how the scoring system operates.

For example, a 'reading' score might test:

- ✓ individual word reading, where there are no contextual clues meaning the child has to recognise the whole word or decode it phonetically;
- ✓ reading comprehension, where a child has to select an answer having read a sentence or passage;
- ✓ a miscue analysis identifying the specific kinds of errors made when reading and their impact on comprehension.

One of the best ways to fully understand any test is to attempt it. First-hand knowledge is perhaps the most useful and quickest insight into the nature of the challenge.

Having an understanding of how tests are scored is essential to a child's learning. Bearing in mind our previous comments about confusing jargon, it is worth knowing how a level, a raw score, a standardised score or a grade has been arrived at. Ultimately the score is simply a shorthand to better know and understand the nature of strengths and weaknesses.

Finally, it is also essential to understand how scores relate to the classroom. Understanding the impact of a baseline score on classroom learning means it's easier to make adjustments to expectations, to look for incremental progress rather than huge leaps that close gaps.

2. Keeping track of 'Plan'

Having carried out an assessment of a pupil's learning difficulties, it follows that the next stage is to 'Plan' and identify a set of strategies to help them progress. In practice, SENCOs very often make this plan and set targets related to specific needs.

As the expectation of all teachers is that they should be prepared to teach all pupils with SEND, it is desirable that they would be involved in this planning process. Class teachers are encouraged to be involved to embed SEND support within the child's daily classroom experience, enabling them to be included in all of their lessons. This kind of individual planning by class teachers is more common in primary settings, as the lack of frequent contact with subject teachers can make this more difficult during the secondary phase. One solution to include a wide range of teachers is to ensure Individual Education Plan (IEP)/Individual Learning Plan (ILP) targets relate to a child's cross-curricular skills, rather than individual subjects. It is then for classroom teachers, in any phase, to apply these cross-curricular targets to their own classroom expectations. After all, 'core deficits' are cross-curricular.

TAs can play a helpful and constructive role in contributing to setting these targets for the pupil. Often, they are the professionals working most frequently, and consistently, with identified pupils. TAs get to see, first hand, the impact of core deficits in each subject of the curriculum.

If TAs are prompted to notice and recall information about how children are coping in relation to the 'core deficits', expectations can be frequently and accurately updated.

The Code does not offer any specific details in terms of the practical application of the Plan stage of the Graduated Approach. The most common approach is to plan support through identifying a set of personalised targets and strategies referred to in IEPs/ILPs, both of which schools are no longer under a duty to provide.

However, in order for a TA to conduct any meaningful day to day tracking, it is necessary for them to have sight of a pupil's baseline data and IEP. In order to implement and contribute to the plan, schools usually ask TAs for oral feedback, lesson- or pupil-centred notes. The level of detail in terms of what is known about a child's learning difficulties will vary enormously. Pupils with EHCPs, and even those without, may have a significant history of diagnostic data. This may come from the school itself, or from external agencies including specialist teachers, educational psychologists, speech and language therapists and occupational therapists. The job of digesting and synthesising this into a school-based plan is less likely to be the responsibility of a TA; nevertheless, having some familiarity with this history is doubtless an advantage, especially in relation to the recommendations it makes for classroom support.

Formats for planning

The Specialist Report Digest is a simple format a TA can use to make useful notes about recommendations made by an external agency or clinician.

TAs support pupils with no identification, those identified as 'SEND support' and those with EHCPS. TAs are asked to make notes about their support and its impact in a variety of different ways but require a structure and a language for this that places the child, and not themselves, at the centre.

The formats in Tables 6.1 to 6.3 prompt TAs to consult with the baseline data irrespective of the categorisation of the child.

Table 6.1 Specialist Report Digest

Date	Report Type	Pupil Name
Notes about baselines		
Subject specific concerns		
Cognitive strengths		
Recommendations about the use of specific materials, books or technology		
Additional notes		

Table 6.2 Getting Ready to Support Pupils with an EHCP

Name of Pupil				
Preparation	**Yes**	**No**	**Information/ Action**	**Date**
Have I read the description of needs?				
Have I read the agreed outcomes?				
Are there any specific adjustments to be made to language?				
Am I aware of and competent to use any assistive technology (radio-mic, etc.)?				
Are there adjustments to be made to the environment?				
What additional or alternative resources are necessary?				
Are there adjustments to be made to the curriculum, content or pace?				
Are there clear next steps towards EHC objectives for pupils this term?				
Have I introduced myself to and agreed a way to communicate with the pupil?				
Are there additional interventions or programmes I can offer to support this pupil?				
Have I met the relevant teaching staff?				
Have we agreed an agenda for in-class support?				
How and when do I feed back on progress?				
Do I have a role in review meetings and parental liaison?				
Do I meet external specialists, health, social care, etc.?				

Table 6.3 Planning for Pupils on SEND Support

Questions	**Yes**	**No**	**Action Response**
Have I consulted the SEND register?			
How many pupils with SEND support am I supporting?			
Have I consulted their baseline data?			
What are the primary areas of need?			
Do I need to modify my language?			
Do they need any additional or alternative resources?			
Is there an agreed agenda for in-class support?			

3. Keeping track of 'Do'

In its simplest form, the 'Do' stage of the Graduated Approach consists of whatever is involved in supporting progress towards the agreed targets that have been set in the Plan stage. This is often where the TA comes into their own, as they provide daily support to identified pupils.

Working with teachers in the classroom

Most of the Do stage of the Graduated Approach will take place within the classroom, as the TA works alongside identified pupils. Hopefully, it is clear from the previous sections on planning that familiarity with baseline data and targets is essential. Everyone, including the pupil, needs to have a clear understanding of the expectations placed upon them and the support they can expect from their TAs.

TAs are often deployed by the SENCO or classroom teachers and therefore have limited control in terms of who they are asked to support and in what context. In the best-case scenario, this deployment is made with some acknowledgement of experience, specialist knowledge, areas of interest and recent training. However, we know that schools have to react and respond quickly as things change and events take over. (We are writing this in lockdown!) It may be that the best laid plans have to be adapted. TAs may change class, pupils or year groups at any point during the academic year. However, being ready to step into a new challenge requires some preparation, if it is to be successful.

In such situations, the 'In-class Support Agenda', featured in Table 6.4, translates the considerations of **DR KEEPIT** into a basic agreement amongst the class teacher, the TA and the pupil. It acts as a prompt to a structured but bespoke conversation about in-class support that reduces the need for constant liaison. Once completed, the agenda provides a set of agreed mutual expectations and a clear plan for working collaboratively around the child. This agenda can then be modified as things change and progress. In working with the teacher to agree this agenda, any TA can apply the principles of **DR KEEPIT** to inform practice, enabling them to support the pupil in an effective way, in any setting.

There is a distinct advantage to pupils in using the **DR KEEPIT** structure to address their learning needs. This well-informed and empathetic approach can also benefit the TA/teacher relationship. Since the initial publication of The Code in 2015, much has been made of the responsibility of teachers to include pupils with SEND in their lessons. Unfortunately, teachers have been afforded no more time to train or indeed to enact this responsibility. TAs, teachers and SENCOs, up and down the country, talk to us about the same concerns – they need more training and more time to talk to each other. The problem is without a manageable and easily communicated plan for these conversations, time alone is not enough to address their concerns.

The agenda set out here should cover a wide range of settings and pupil needs but may well require personalisation in order to produce an explicit agreement about a way of working within a particular lesson or with a particular pupil. By addressing this agenda point by point, the TA and the teacher can have a conversation that establishes a way of working together that is clear to both.

We spent some time thinking about roles in respect to using this agenda – is it for the TA to lead on this, or should they simply work to the expectations of their colleagues? We came to the conclusion that ultimately a TA makes an offer of support, to a pupil or to a colleague based on their knowledge and experience – everyone has a way of working that is unique to them. This agenda is simply an explicit, written version of that offer.

By making the nature of the support offer explicit, professionals (and pupils) are less likely to make and rely upon assumptions about each other's way of working. In our experience, it is when we make these assumptions that misunderstandings can arise and feelings can be hurt. When we 'assume', we risk starting on the back foot and approach this relationship by correcting mistakes and revealing concerns than by being clear and open in the first place.

The 'In-class Support Agenda', like all tools in this book, is fully editable and can be adapted to include more detail to record resources and elaborate on certain aspects of the agreement. In the online resources, we provide two versions of this document. One has an additional column to record the comments from pupils.

Table 6.4 In-Class Support Agenda

	In-Class Support Agenda	**Details**
D	Pupils know how to get my attention.	
D	I check in with open questions.	
D	I repeat instructions using the same language as the teacher.	
R	I provide visual cues and additional resources in advance of the lesson.	
R	I provide visual cues and additional resources as required in the lesson.	
R	I prompt pupils to make use of appropriate technology and software.	
K	I highlight and emphasise key points.	
E	I share information about learning.	
E	I am clear about the rewards and sanctions I can offer.	
E	I encourage risk-taking in learning.	
E	I enable teacher engagement/involvement with my target pupils.	

	In-Class Support Agenda	Details
P	I circulate and avoid sitting with one pupil for extended periods.	
I	I have a toolkit to support working memory.	
I	I have a sensory toolkit for supporting pupils with DCD and SID.	
T	I chunk tasks.	

Explanation of In-Class Support Agenda items

As you can see, each agenda item relates to one letter of **DR KEEPIT**. *For more information, please refer to the appropriate section in Chapter 5.*

- **Pupils know how to get my attention** – this is about managing interruptions and communicating with a pupil during the flow of the lesson. Are pupils going to employ a signal to attract the TAs attention; can they talk to the TA when the teacher is talking; what about volume and distractions?
- **I check in with open questions** – TAs are likely to take a key role in checking understanding. It is useful to discuss how and when the teacher becomes involved in this.
- **I repeat instructions using the same language as the teacher** – repetition, prompting and reminders can form a significant part of the TA role; however, it's important that we consolidate understanding and reduce confusion; the way we approach this task is, therefore, worth taking a moment to consider.
- **I provide visual cues and additional resources in advance of the lesson** – hopefully this prompts a discussion about the relevance of materials, resources and technology so that TAs can familiarise themselves in advance of lessons and help to guide pupils towards materials and tools that support learning.
- **I provide visual cues and additional resources as required in the lesson** – it might be possible to have a 'low-tech tool kit' of helpful items to support working memory – this can help to create visual cues as the lesson progresses or provide pupils with opportunity to manage this process themselves.
- **I prompt pupils to make use of appropriate technology and software** – this might be in the form of making sure laptops are charged and ready, understanding software that supports writing or mind-mapping, prompting pupils to use reading pens or coloured glasses – technology that allows children to be more independent in their learning is worth encouraging.

- **I highlight and emphasise key points** – this is a prompt to ensure teachers and TAs share this information and check in with each other concerning the key points of the lesson.
- **I share information about learning** – utilising the tools in this chapter for planning and recording support. It is useful to ensure that TAs and teachers have realistic and agreed points of contact for sharing.
- **I am clear about the rewards and sanctions I can offer** – behaviour management can be a point of sensitivity between teachers and TAs. It is necessary to have a conversation where decisions are made about protocol and authority.
- **I encourage risk-taking in learning** – this invites a check-in with teachers about aspirations and expectations – is there agreement about what represents ambitious goals for the pupils supported?
- **I enable teacher engagement/involvement with my target pupils** – this is a conversation that recognises the pupil's need for direct input and support from their teachers; how is it best to facilitate this?
- **I circulate and avoid sitting with one pupil for extended periods** – making sure that issues of proximity are addressed is essential in allowing pupils an increasing degree of independence. Sometimes it can be uncomfortable for TAs to position themselves away from their pupils as they may appear to be disengaged; managing this proactively with the teacher allows everyone to work with purpose and confidence.
- **I have a toolkit to support working memory** – see 'low-tech toolkit' on page 69.
- **I have a sensory toolkit for supporting pupils with coordination and sensory disorders** – see 'Sensory toolkit' on page 39.
- **I chunk tasks** – discussing how a set of learning outcomes might be successfully broken down or prioritised allows for a conversation about pace and refers back to the issues of key points (page 71).

Interventions led by TAs outside of the classroom

TAs are often asked by the SENCO, or the class teacher, to work with a small group of children or an individual pupil on a specific intervention. Sometimes these interventions are specifically focused on subject knowledge to reinforce prior learning, or as over-learning to embed knowledge and skills. TAs are also often provided training in the delivery of a prescribed intervention programme. There are numerous intervention packages available on the market covering literacy, numeracy, social skills and working memory, to name but a few. The Education Endowment Foundation's (EEF, 2020) *Teaching and Learning Toolkit* provides a list of interventions and their proposed value and impact on a child. If delivering a 'bought in' intervention programme is part of the TA's role, it's important to feel confident about its purpose, the method of delivery and the timeline for review. Preparation to lead the intervention may involve working alongside teachers or the SENCO, shadowing an experienced TA or practicing it at home or at school before it is delivered to pupils.

In order to feed back on pupil progress and the impact of any intervention, it's also important to form an understanding of how it is assessed and to be clear about scoring. It's likely that pupils will have questions about their performance and progress during lessons. In this way, any feedback will be accurate and consistent.

Children may be difficult to engage and motivate depending on the timing and content of the intervention session. As the professional in charge during these interventions, it is really helpful if you can record and discuss pupil feedback with the SENCO or class teacher to agree an approach to managing the session, and to look at the transfer of skills into the wider curriculum.

To get the best out of interventions it's useful to consider:

- **Appropriate settings** – is the intervention taking place somewhere with adequate space, resources, light, sound levels and privacy?
- **Multi-sensory** – does the lesson stimulate the senses and involve the child actively in their learning?
- **Time management** – is there enough time for everyone to arrive, settle and complete the tasks, and does the session take place at a time where children are not concerned about missing out on a club, game, break, lunch or other aspects of school they enjoy?
- **Frequency** – is the session a regular part of their routine?
- **Conventions** – do they know what the TA's role is in the session if this is different in some way from the in-class role? Do they know how to address the TA and how to behave?
- **Safeguarding** – has safeguarding training taken place enabling the TA to feel confident in managing pupils independently? Small groups can affect relationships and impact the way pupils behave.
- **Be positive** – does the TA have a positive approach to this session in that its purpose and benefit is understood?
- **Relevance** – is the intervention relevant to the pupil and their profile of needs?
- **Resources** – are there sufficient resources to deliver the intervention as designed?

If any of the areas in the interventions list are of concern, make a note of the issues and talk to the SENCO.

The Intervention Grid

Table 6.5 is an Intervention Grid which can be used to record and to track pupil progress for interventions led independently by TAs. It can be adapted for use with individuals or small groups. It also acts as a register of attendance which can be helpful when reviewing pupil progress. If completed consistently, it can be useful evidence in the 'Review' stage of the Graduated Approach.

Table 6.5 Intervention Grid

Group or Pupil Name	Year Group	Intervention	Small Group/ Individual	Start Date	End Date
Date	Session Number	Key learning for the session			
Pupil's engagement with the task					
Any additional resources/strategies used					
Pupil's achievements in the session					
Areas where the pupil struggled					
Outcomes from the session					
Important points for next session					

4. Keeping track of 'Review'

Keeping a written record of activities is important if TAs are going to contribute to reports, reviews and meeting with external agencies. However, records shouldn't be a full-time job; we are no fans of endless written notes. When we are recording our professional duties or planning it should be effective and efficient; we shouldn't need to reinvent the processes over and over again and the record should be a prompt to the key issues.

The Review stage of the Graduated Approach is an opportunity to look at which targets have been achieved for the pupil. It also acts to inform the new targets that are set. If the Plan process established SMART targets, this should be a relatively straightforward process. The SENCO will normally take the lead in such reviews. Usually targets are set half-term or termly; having worked towards this a Review is likely to happen up to three times in the school year. Whilst Annual Reviews form part of the Graduated Approach for pupils with EHCPs, all pupils with SEND should have regular progress reviews according to this cycle.

SMART Targets should be:

Specific – to an identified area of need;

Measurable – set a clear outcome for the end of the intervention;

Attainable – it should be within the pupil's capabilities to achieve the target, with or without support;

Relevant – designed to move the pupil on in their learning;

Time-bound – should be achieved within a clear time frame.

Annual Reviews

All pupils with an EHCP are entitled to a formal Annual Review process, which involves all external agencies and key support staff. The review considers all aspects of the EHCP and has a particular focus on establishing how the special educational provision is enabling pupil progress. A representative from the LA should be present at an Annual Review, as it remains the duty of the LA to arrange the provision in the EHCP and therefore to monitor its impact. The minutes of the review, including any change to circumstances or to needs, should be with the LA within 10 days. It is then for the LA to update the EHCP accordingly. In practice, LAs struggle to attend all reviews and do not necessarily update EHCPs on an annual basis – Annual Review minutes and the updated targets for pupils that they contain are an essential additional reference when planning to support a pupil.

How can TAs contribute to Review?

Primarily, the Review stage identifies whether the provision is working effectively and that as a result, the pupil is progressing towards the goals set in the Plan stage.

If TAs are using the In-Class Support Agenda to track pupils or, indeed, the EHCP of SEND support planning documents, it's likely that they will have specific information about how their role and approach to providing support is working – this can then be cross-referenced with a pupil's curricular attainment to provide detailed information about the impact of provision. Feedback from the Intervention Grid can also contribute to this process.

Using the In-Class Support Agenda to support pupil voice in Review

The **DR KEEPIT** principles can be a useful tool in reviewing how a child is progressing through their targets and managing their learning. A modified In-Class Support Agenda follows in Table 6.6 with an additional column to note pupil voice.

It's possible to complete the pupil response section as frequently as necessary. This can be done while working alongside the pupil in class, following a discussion or observation or during a one-to-one session.

Each agenda item can be used as a prompt to invite feedback about the nature and impact of the support provided. It is sometimes helpful to complete the process independently as a self-assessment and then compare pupil or class teacher responses. This can be further enriched by reference to work produced, marking and assessment feedback.

Table 6.6 Modified In-Class Support Agenda

	In-Class Support Agenda	**Details**	**Pupil Response**
D	Pupils know how to get my attention.		Is the pupil asking for help, asking questions?
D	I check in with open questions.		Is the pupil able to have a conversation about learning?
D	I repeat instructions using the same language as the teacher.		Is this necessary, useful, improving?
R	I provide visual cues and additional resources in advance of the lesson.		Examples of use
R	I provide visual cues and additional resources as required in the lesson.		Examples of use
R	I prompt pupils to make use of appropriate technology and software.		Examples of use
K	I highlight and emphasise key points.		How and is it effective? What impact is there?
E	I share information about learning.		
E	I am clear about the rewards and sanctions I can offer.		Strategies for behaviour management and celebrating success
E	I encourage risk-taking in learning.		Examples
E	I enable teacher engagement/ involvement with my target pupils.		Is the pupil working with the teacher?
P	I circulate and avoid sitting with one pupil for extended periods.		
I	I have a toolkit to support working memory.		Is it being used – which elements and with what success?
I	I have a sensory toolkit for supporting pupils with DCD and SID.		Is it being used – which elements and with what success?
T	I chunk tasks.		How and with what impact?

Summary

How can TAs contribute to the Graduated Approach for pupils with SEND?

- A school may have its own unique way of applying the Graduated Approach in making provision for pupils with SEND.
- The system describes a cycle of activity; Assess-Plan-Do-Review, in which all professionals participate.
- The Graduated Approach is evidence based. All planning and provision of support for pupils should be subject to review and the outcome of that review be the basis of ongoing planning and provision.
- It is likely that pupils are at different stages of this cycle at any one time, as needs arise in between cycles of assessment. This can make it difficult for TAs to keep track and feed back on progress.
- TAs play key roles in planning and making provision and in feedback at review.
- To keep track at the Assess stage a TA needs access to information about a pupil's performance across the curriculum. This includes having an understanding of any baseline data about basic skills.
- To keep track at the Plan stage it can help to be familiar with the targets set for pupils on IEPs or ILPs.
- This may be more complex in reference to EHCPs or the recommendations made in specialist reports. Using the formats on page 117 and page 118 can assist in managing this process.
- Keeping track of the Do stage can be supported by developing an In-Class Support Agenda with the teacher and using this as a prompt for monitoring strategies and pupil responses. See page 120.
- Thinking carefully about working to deliver interventions includes consideration of appropriate settings, multi-sensory techniques, time management, frequency, conventions, safeguarding, positivity, relevance and resources. The grid on page 124 is a useful tool for this monitoring.
- Keeping track of Review is made more straightforward by recording and planning, using the structures suggested previously, as instead of producing retrospective summaries, TAs can use day-to-day feedback to report on the impact of support in terms of pupil progress.
- To include pupils in Review, see the pupil response document on page 126.

Resources

Table 6.1 Specialist Report Digest

Date	Report Type	Pupil Name
Notes about baselines		
Subject specific concerns		
Cognitive strengths		
Recommendations about the use of specific materials, books or technology		
Additional notes		

Table 6.2 Getting Ready to Support Pupils with an EHCP

Name of Pupil				
Preparation	**Yes**	**No**	**Information/Action**	**Date**
Have I read the description of needs?				
Have I read the agreed outcomes?				
Are there any specific adjustments to be made to language?				
Am I aware of and competent to use any assistive technology (radio-mic, etc.)?				
Are there adjustments to be made to the environment?				
What additional or alternative resources are necessary?				
Are there adjustments to be made to the curriculum, content or pace?				
Are there clear next steps towards EHC objectives for pupils this term?				

Name of Pupil				
Preparation	**Yes**	**No**	**Information/Action**	**Date**
Have I introduced myself to and agreed a way to communicate with the pupil?				
Are there additional interventions or programmes I can offer to support this pupil?				
Have I met the relevant teaching staff?				
Have we agreed an agenda for in-class support?				
How and when do I feed back on progress?				
Do I have a role in review meetings and parental liaison?				
Do I meet external specialists, health, social care, etc.?				

Table 6.3 Planning for Pupils on SEND Support

Questions	Yes	No	Action Response
Have I consulted the SEND register?			
How many pupils with SEN support am I supporting?			
Have I consulted their baseline data?			
What are the primary areas of need?			
Do I need to modify my language?			
Do they need any additional or alternative resources?			
Is there an agreed agenda for in-class support?			

Table 6.4 In-Class Support Agenda

	In-Class Support Agenda	**Details**
D	Pupils know how to get my attention.	
D	I check in with open questions.	
D	I repeat instructions using the same language as the teacher.	
R	I provide visual cues and additional resources in advance of the lesson.	
R	I provide visual cues and additional resources as required in the lesson.	
R	I prompt pupils to make use of appropriate technology and software.	
K	I highlight and emphasise key points.	
E	I share information about learning.	

(*Continued*)

Table 6.4 (Continued)

	In-Class Support Agenda	Details
E	I am clear about the rewards and sanctions I can offer.	
E	I encourage risk-taking in learning.	
E	I enable teacher engagement/involvement with my target pupils.	
P	I circulate and avoid sitting with one pupil for extended periods.	
I	I have a toolkit to support working memory.	
I	I have a sensory toolkit for supporting pupils with DCD and SID.	
T	I chunk tasks.	

Table 6.5 Intervention Grid

Group or Pupil Name	**Year Group**	**Intervention**	**Small Group/ Individual**	**Start Date**	**End Date**
Date	**Session Number**	**Key learning for the session**			
Pupil's engagement with the task					
Any additional resources/ strategies used					
Pupil's achievements in the session					
Areas where the pupil struggled					
Outcomes from the session					
Important points for next session					

Table 6.6 Modified In-Class Support Agenda

	In-Class Support Agenda	Details	Pupil Response
D	Pupils know how to get my attention.		
D	I check in with open questions.		
D	I repeat instructions using the same language as the teacher.		
R	I provide visual cues and additional resources in advance of the lesson.		
R	I provide visual cues and additional resources as required in the lesson.		
R	I prompt pupils to make use of appropriate technology and software.		
K	I highlight and emphasise key points.		
E	I share information about learning.		

	In-Class Support Agenda	Details	Pupil Response
E	I am clear about the rewards and sanctions I can offer.		
E	I encourage risk-taking in learning.		
E	I enable teacher engagement/ involvement with my target pupils.		
P	I circulate and avoid sitting with one pupil for extended periods.		
I	I have a toolkit to support working memory.		
I	I have a sensory toolkit for supporting pupils with DCD and SID.		
T	I chunk tasks.		

7 What do TAs need to know about identifying learners with SEND?

The Needs Matrix

What is the role of the TA in this process?

'In identifying a child as needing SEN support the class or subject teacher, working with the SENCO, should carry out a clear analysis of the pupil's needs' (DFE & DoH, 2015, p. 100). The Code sets out roles for the SENCO and teachers in this respect but does not make any specific demands on TAs. However, in practice, TAs are often involved by their colleagues in this process. Depending on experience and the frequency of their contact with the pupils, teachers and SENCOs often consult TAs in building a picture of a child's learning needs or indeed in considering making ongoing referrals.

The Code encourages schools to consider the following in identifying SEND:

- ✓ Slow or slowing progress rates and attainment gaps;
- ✓ The impact of High Quality Teaching HQT and differentiation on those rates and gaps;
- ✓ The impact of additional interventions and additional teaching;
- ✓ The desired outcome;
- ✓ Sustained concern in respect of progress and attainment;
- ✓ The fact that age appropriate attainment does not preclude a learning difficulty;
- ✓ All data available on the child, including views of child and family.

The list of considerations leans heavily toward slow progress and attainment, and underachievement as drivers for identification. However, the last bullet point reminds us that not all learning difficulties manifest in this way. With such a broad remit and loose set of criteria, how do we know what to notice?

Whilst we wouldn't encourage TAs to think in terms of diagnosing difficulties or making judgements and describing labels, they have a role to play in considering why children might react as they do in the classroom environment. In many ways, the most important contribution a TA can make to this identification process is in noticing the child and their responses, whatever they might be. In the everyday classroom experience, the 'noticing' part often passes very swiftly, before a judgement of some kind is made and action taken to address, reprimand or instruct. What we are advocating here is a more protracted period of observation where we look at a variety of factors over time, in different situations and from more than one perspective before we move to the next step, remembering that a number of different and possibly unhelpful behaviours may have a root cause that is less obvious.

Obviously, if a child is doing something that may harm themselves, or someone else, there is no time for observation and action needs to come first. The school's policies on safeguarding and bullying will have substantial references on how to manage any behaviour that is of immediate concern.

This section is focused on how to notice and what to notice in the quieter moments; how a child approaches their classroom experience in terms of attention, language, literacy, processing, peer relationships and motivation.

In offering the Needs Matrix structure, we are hoping to guide TAs working in busy classrooms through a list of considerations that may prove to be indicators of undiagnosed learning difficulties.

The Needs Matrix can be used in a variety of ways. It is principally a prompt sheet to invite observations of specifics, rather than to invite general comments on pupil progress. Instead of looking at broad strokes like attainment and progress over time, or at baseline data, like reading and spelling ages, it invites the user to consider the details; how learning is happening rather than what is being learned. After all, we all learn in different ways and at different rates; becoming aware of what works for us is part of making good choices for the future. For example, we find that writing in a quiet house, early in the morning, before the noise of the day and the distractions begin, is more successful than working late at night.

The Needs Matrix is designed to focus our awareness of a child's approach to learning and thereby helps support the child's self-awareness, so that they can make the most of the skills and talents they have. Admittedly, there are myriad checklists for individual specific learning difficulties, for dyslexia, dyscalculia, traits of autism, etc.; however, based on our experience and on current research, we know that it is likely that a number of SpLDs occur simultaneously and that children may experience a unique combination of issues. We have, therefore, brought together descriptors of traits from a number of high-incidence SpLDs into one format; hopefully, the jargon is translated into easily recognisable features. We are attempting to describe the child when learning, not fit their traits to a label.

The aim of using the Needs Matrix is to create a greater degree of objectivity, a pair of fresh eyes, when providing feedback about a pupil's approach to learning. TAs are often invited to make comments and offer their notes to be used in support of decision making. In our experience, without a clear structure, these notes can be rather too subjective, and in fact, can tell you more about the person responsible for writing them than they do about the subject of the observation.

While we are beginning to accept that individuals think and process differently, that we are a neurodiverse species, in schools we still think of teaching and learning in terms of what is a typical and an atypical response. At the moment, our system to address neurodiversity and to provide additional features and additional funding is dependent on the identification of a specific disorder or learning difficulty. It looks like it will take some time for schools to catch up with academics and neuroscientists who are moving away from this deficit model.

Using the Needs Matrix in school

The checklist features 45 suggested barriers to learning for the TAs consideration. The section at the top requires the TA to complete the pupil's details and then to rate their current attainment in this setting as below (B), at expected (E) levels or above expectations (A).

Following from this initial information, it's necessary to work down the form, considering each feature describing a barrier to learning 1–45. Once considered, each feature suggested can be rated or removed, depending on relevance. The rating invited is a frequency rating; the question is, to what extent or how frequently is this feature a barrier to classroom learning? A tick in the high rating column suggests that this is a really pervasive issue that greatly hampers a pupil's access to the lesson and their attainment, and a tick in the low rating column means it may still be noticeable but to a lesser extent. The comments section exists for the TA to record details about this feature if that's helpful.

The features explained:

1. **Keeping things in mind** – does the child struggle to remember instructions or other incidental information, including routines, letters and equipment?
2. **Remembering processes and sequences** – despite having listened and followed processes and sequences in the lesson or previously, does the child struggle to retain or replicate sequences and processes that support their work? E.g. months of the year, days of the week, timetables.
3. **Remembering letters and symbols** – does the child fail to recognise, replicate and use letters and symbols?
4. **Plan and do (completing written tasks)** – despite adequate reading and spelling skills, does the child struggle to manage a complete and independent written response (otherwise known as executive function)?
5. **Processing speech sounds** – does the child struggle to identify and replicate speech sounds?
6. **Remembering sounds** – does the child struggle to recall speech sounds?
7. **Matching phoneme to grapheme** – does the child struggle to match letters to speech sounds when reading and/or writing?
8. **Slow pace** – does the child work at a slower pace than their peers and do they fail to complete tasks within the time allotted?

9. **Reading (accuracy/speed/fluency/comprehension)** – is the child able to read the lesson materials and resources independently? Is there a standardised score for reading available?
10. **Spelling** – does the child struggle to spell regular and high frequency words consistently? Is there a standardised score for spelling available?
11. **Laterality** – does the child have a dominant hand – right or left?
12. **Core stability** – does the child struggle to maintain an upright seated position? Do they wriggle and move around excessively or uncomfortably in their seat?
13. **Fine and gross motor skills** – does the child struggle to grip or manipulate a pen or pencil? Are they able to use tools to measure, draw and make?
14. **Proprioception** – does the child struggle to manage their body in space? Do they bump into objects or people or misjudge distances, pressure and force?
15. **Co-ordination** – does the child struggle to co-ordinate their movements when carrying out everyday activities; unpacking a bag, dressing, buttoning, tying, catching and throwing, etc.?
16. **Balance** – does the child struggle to balance when carrying out everyday activities?
17. **Concepts of number** – does the child struggle to retain numerical values?
18. **Algebra** – does the child struggle to manage symbols and codes in mathematics?
19. **Complex calculations** – does the child struggle to retain processes or sequences in making calculations?
20. **Proximity** – does the child stand either too close or too far from other people or objects?
21. **Relating to peers** – does the child find it difficult to make and/or sustain appropriate relationships with peers?
22. **Appropriate responses** – does the child struggle to respond appropriately in conversations with others either in terms of content, tone or register?
23. **Awareness of social cues** – does the child pick up on non-verbal cues, facial expressions and gestures?
24. **Range of interest** – does the child have a narrower than usual range of interest?
25. **Eye contact** – does the child struggle to make or sustain eye contact when engaged with others?
26. **Social understanding and interaction** – does the child struggle to pick up on social cues?
27. **Non-verbal and verbal communication** – does the child struggle with both verbal and non-verbal communication?
28. **Imagination and flexible thinking** – is it difficult to engage the child in imaginative thinking? Do they struggle with departures from routine or do they interpret figurative language literally?

29 **Blurting** – does the child struggle to contain a verbal response and make contributions spontaneously or inappropriately?
30 **Turn taking** – does the child struggle to wait for their turn or recognise turn-taking unless prompted?
31 **Lack of participation** – is the child passive, distracted or withdrawn from activities?
32 **Fidgeting** – does the child frequently play, pick or fiddle with objects in their environment, including their own body, clothing and belongings?
33 **Day dreaming** – is the child regularly focused on something other than the speaker, resources, object of the lesson?
34 **Focus** – does the child lose focus more frequently than their peers?
35 **Reluctance to switch activities** – is the child often unwilling to move on in their learning?
36 **Difficulty sitting** – is a child often uncomfortable and irritable when seated?
37 **Out of seat** – does the child spontaneously move around the classroom, school or available space?
38 **Tapping and drumming** – does the child tap fingers and other objects so that they are audible to themselves and others?
39 **Dislike of dirty hands** – does the child react adversely to messy play, cooking, painting or other activities in which the hands become discoloured, wet or sticky?
40 **Excessive pressure** – does the child break pencils and pens or other equipment or push so hard as to tear or emboss paper when working?
41 **Receptive language** – does the child struggle to understand, interpret or follow instructions and information shared orally?
42 **Expressive language** – does the child struggle to express their thoughts or opinions at an age appropriate level?
43 **Pragmatics of speech** – does the child struggle to participate in conversations?
44 **Semantics** – does the child find it difficult to understand the meaning of words or to use the correct words to express an idea?
45 **Articulation** – does the child struggle to make the appropriate speech sounds?

The information recorded in the Needs Matrix can be used to:

✓ Provide a one-off observation of a child following a concern or referral;
✓ Provide a template for a number of teachers or TAs to compare their observations;
✓ Be a tool for self-reflection for a pupil, to use independently or while being supported by a member of staff;
✓ Compare a pupil's behaviour and responses over time;

- ✓ Compare a pupil's behaviour and responses at different times of the day, in different subjects, in different settings or when being taught by different teachers;
- ✓ Compare a pupil's behaviour in the classroom and in non-contact time; play, clubs, sports, lunch and assembly;
- ✓ Have an evidenced-based conversation with the SENCO or classroom teacher;
- ✓ Inform a conversation with the child and their parents;
- ✓ Support a referral to an external agency;
- ✓ Track the impact of support on specific areas of difficulty;
- ✓ Reinforce knowledge about SpLDs and create a common terminology amongst the staff.

Collating and using the feedback

Whether working independently or in collaboration with colleagues, once completed it's necessary to review and collate feedback, looking carefully at which features are apparent and how they are rated. The feedback can then be presented in a more concise form. A digest of the form can be created by simply deleting any irrelevant areas, thereby creating a list of priorities.

If there is more than one form to review, the simplest way to approach this is to complete a tally of the ratings for each feature. While this is likely to present a set of priorities, it's also important to explore any anomalies. Pupils may well present very differently in different settings and while we might be, first and foremost, concerned with identifying difficulties, much can be learned from identifying what is working well and using this knowledge to build on pupil strengths.

The next step might be further investigation on the part of the teacher or SENCO, or it may be that it leads you to amend your **in-class agenda** to include some support for the pupil. Clearly, this level of detail is likely to be useful should you be required to be involved in ongoing monitoring of the pupil or in planning to provide support.

Using the Needs Matrix with existing pupils with SEND

It's entirely possible to use the Needs Matrix (Table 7.1) to monitor pupils whose needs have already been identified. In preparation for a period of review, or even an Annual Review, it can be very useful to have a detailed snapshot of a pupil's way of working. Further, it is possible for the needs of pupils with an identified SEND to develop and change; needs arise as children move through the system and as they get older. Looking at pupils with fresh eyes can be essential in future-proofing their support and ensuring we are able to adapt and change our approach as they grow and progress.

Table 7.1 The Needs Matrix

		Please Tick			Comments
Current attainment in your subject		B	E	A	
Rate behaviours affecting learning adversely – there is no need to rate every descriptor		Frequency Rating			
		High	Medium	Low	
1	Keeping things in mind				
2	Remembering processes/ sequences				
3	Remembering letters and symbols				
4	Plan and do (completing written tasks)				
5	Processing speech sounds				
6	Remembering sounds				
7	Matching phoneme to grapheme				
8	Slow pace				
9	Reading – speed/fluency/ comprehension				
10	Spelling				

		Please Tick			Comments
Rate behaviours affecting learning adversely – there is no need to rate every descriptor		**Frequency Rating**			
		High	**Medium**	**Low**	
11	Laterality (right from left)				
12	Core stability				
13	Fine and gross motor skills				
14	Proprioception (awareness of body in space)				
15	Co-ordination				
16	Balance				
17	Concepts of number				
18	Algebra				
19	Complex calculations				
20	Proximity				
21	Relating to peers				
22	Appropriate responses				
23	Awareness of social cues				
24	Range of interests				
25	Eye contact				
26	Social understanding and interaction				
27	Non-verbal and verbal communication				
28	Imagination and flexible thinking				

(*Continued*)

Table 7.1 (Continued)

		Please Tick			Comments
Rate behaviours affecting learning adversely – there is no need to rate every descriptor		**Frequency Rating**			
		High	**Medium**	**Low**	
29	Blurting				
30	Turn taking				
31	Lack of participation				
32	Fidgety				
33	Day dreaming				
34	Focus				
35	Reluctance to switch activities				
36	Difficulty sitting				
37	Out of seat				
38	Taps and drums				
39	Dislikes getting dirty hands				
40	Excessive pressure				
41	Receptive language				
42	Expressive language				
43	Pragmatics				
44	Semantics				
45	Articulation				

Summary

What do TAs need to know about identifying learners with SEND? The Needs Matrix

- TAs often work with teaching staff and the SENCO in supporting the identification of pupils with SEND.
- The Needs Matrix provides a framework for on-going and comparative close observation of pupils' learning habits.
- TAs generally do not have responsibility for the process of identification but may well offer feedback to colleagues due to a high level of contact with pupils.
- The Code sets out a number of specific considerations when identifying SEND in school. These can be found in Chapter 1.
- The Needs Matrix is **not** a diagnostic tool as it does not provide any measures of attainment; it can only be used to notice and gather information about the way a pupil is working.
- Specific learning difficulties often occur in combinations; this is often referred to as co-morbidity.
- Neuroscientists are increasingly defining learning differences in terms of neurodiversity rather than as difficulties or deficits – removing the stigma from identifying the differences in the way humans think and process. In time, this model may replace the current model of typical and atypical learners.
- The Needs Matrix invites the observer to make 45 considerations about a pupil's learning habits and attitudes. How to use it and the features included are explained in detail in the list from page 136.
- The information recorded can be used in a variety of ways to support the identification of SEND.
- It can also be used to monitor a pupil with identified learning difficulties, to review and feed into on-going planning.

Resources

Table 7.1 The Needs Matrix

		Please Tick			Comments
Current attainment in your subject		B	E	A	
Rate behaviours affecting learning adversely – there is no need to rate every descriptor		Frequency Rating			
		High	Medium	Low	
1	Keeping things in mind				
2	Remembering processes/ sequences				
3	Remembering letters and symbols				
4	Plan and do (completing written tasks)				
5	Processing speech sounds				
6	Remembering sounds				
7	Matching phoneme to grapheme				
8	Slow pace				
9	Reading – speed/fluency/ comprehension				
10	Spelling				

Rate behaviours affecting learning adversely – there is no need to rate every descriptor		Please Tick			Comments
		Frequency Rating			
		High	Medium	Low	
11	Laterality (right from left)				
12	Core stability				
13	Fine and gross motor skills				
14	Proprioception (awareness of body in space)				
15	Co-ordination				
16	Balance				
17	Concepts of number				
18	Algebra				
19	Complex calculations				
20	Proximity				
21	Relating to peers				
22	Appropriate responses				
23	Awareness of social cues				
24	Range of interests				
25	Eye contact				
26	Social understanding and interaction				
27	Non-verbal and verbal communication				
28	Imagination and flexible thinking				

(*Continued*)

Table 7.1 (Continued)

		Please Tick			Comments
	Rate behaviours affecting learning adversely – there is no need to rate every descriptor	Frequency Rating			
		High	Medium	Low	
29	Blurting				
30	Turn taking				
31	Lack of participation				
32	Fidgety				
33	Day dreaming				
34	Focus				
35	Reluctance to switch activities				
36	Difficulty sitting				
37	Out of seat				
38	Taps and drums				
39	Dislikes getting dirty hands				
40	Excessive pressure				
41	Receptive language				
42	Expressive language				
43	Pragmatics				
44	Semantics				
45	Articulation				

8 The importance of shared practice

Like me (*Abigail Gray*), many TAs begin their work in schools with no specific training and little experience. My early years in school were spent supporting pupils in other people's classrooms. I very quickly understood that often teachers could feel rather vulnerable as a result of having another adult in the room. Being aware of this and working together to establish a professional, co-operative relationship was a constant feature of the role.

Sharing is at the heart of the TA role. Sharing space, sharing information, sharing aims, sharing strategies, sharing the burden and sharing the success. Without communication, collaboration and, above all, respect between professionals and between professionals and pupils, it's almost impossible to function as a TA, let alone succeed.

Without acknowledgement of this often complex set of dynamics, it is difficult for TAs to develop consistent, professional relationships. The disparities that exist between teachers and TAs are often glossed over. However, they exist and can cause tension and division in the staffroom and have a negative impact for pupils. The distinctions between teachers and TAs are often most visible in terms of authority, and certainly in terms of pay. TAs vary enormously in terms of their experience and specialist knowledge, but they exist within management structures that have limited capacity to recognise this. This can create a challenging set of dynamics, especially where experienced and well qualified TAs are supporting inexperienced but highly paid teachers.

Finding ways to address the nuances here is not easy; very often it falls to TAs themselves or SENCOs to find solutions. Some TAs are part of a large team and, therefore, have a group of peers and a line manager with whom they meet regularly. However, in the majority of schools with part-time TAs the logistics of getting a team together can be challenging. This can result in a very different experience for different members of the same team. Whilst some are integrated into a supportive network, others can be isolated without immediate support.

It's also important to recognise different kinds of sharing and manage this process appropriately. We might share when we need help and ideas, advice on how to deal with a misunderstanding, or new strategies to support a pupil. We might also share when we just need to breathe out and vent frustration; this kind of sharing really needs to take place somewhere other than the staffroom. Unfortunately, it can be difficult to find a private space in schools to be angry or sad or to let off steam when necessary.

Our approach to support a healthy feedback culture and a professional approach to sharing with colleagues is a simple one. By using the In-Class Support Agenda or other planning tools, it's often possible to pre-empt misunderstanding by addressing the practical aspects of the in-class role very deliberately. It's not uncommon for collaborators to disagree, but the way to resolution is to stick to the facts and consider what has been agreed upon.

It might help to do the following when addressing setbacks and criticism:

* **Collect information** – listen actively to all feedback. It is not easy to do this. However, unless a problem is described fully and clear to all parties, there is no hope of finding and establishing a solution.
* **Note concerns** – record what is known; facts, not opinions. Don't rely on memory; keep track of what you know rather than what you think or feel.
* **Consider context** – are there other important facts about this situation that have yet to come to light? It may be that there is a key piece of information missing, unknown or overlooked that can shed light on and unpick an issue.
* **Manage emotions** – is it necessary to wait, or cool down and reflect before commenting or taking action? Neurologically, it's not possible to use the rational part of our brains effectively when we are in the midst of a strong emotional response and adrenalin is at work.
* **Get support** – is there someone who can advise impartially? Make sure this is a person who is likely to listen to and understand the issue. A friend or loved one may not be able to see the situation objectively.
* **Solution focus** – what's the looked-for outcome? Sometimes we get lost in describing a problem; unnecessary repetition can lead to unnecessary escalation. Note what it is that you want or need and why. Then pose the question: is this solution in the best interest of the pupil?
* **School policy** – does the school's policy documentation refer to this situation? Is it important to share this or refer to it?
* **Contract** – is this situation covered in your contract of employment or the staff handbook?

Support networks

Good practice in sharing facilitates sharing good practice. Essentially this involves finding time, and at least one other person who is willing to collaborate. Finding a collaborator – or better still, some collaborators – can really help in creating new perspectives, opportunities and solutions.

The one lesson we can share here, as co-authors, is that working together is more fun, less stressful and more productive than working alone.

Whilst it is necessary to let off steam, enjoy down-time and take a moment for oneself, it's also a good idea to take care of the stresses associated with TA life more proactively. Getting into good habits in terms of sharing can help in problem solving and boost morale. If you can find 15 or 20 minutes to get together in a pair or a group, why not try one of the following activities designed to do both:

* **Build self-esteem** – sit in a circle and write down one thing you value about the person sitting to your right – pass on the paper and watch the effect!
* **Share knowledge and skills** – choose an article/video about SEND that interests you – copy and/or share it and talk about it as a group.
* **Identify support networks** – have a 'concerns box' where you can post questions, worries or queries anonymously – pick one each session and work to a solution. Join a professional association or union.
* **Create a bank of tips and tricks** – have a space where you can post a sticky note with something that went well and build up a collection of ideas and suggestions.
* **Give thanks** – collect and display 'thank you' notes and messages from anyone, yourself included, and read them aloud.

Continuing professional development

TAs can sometimes be left out of the loop in terms of training and miss out on opportunities for professional development. Whether this is due to scheduling issues or pay and conditions, it can result in a rather two-tier approach to professional development for teaching and support staff.

Most schools have systems in place to manage the performance of their employees. A system of appraisal is usual set out in an annual cycle. As well as keeping track of the professional contribution made by an individual according to their role, it can offer an opportunity for reflection on strengths, weaknesses and gaps in knowledge that can be addressed by ongoing education and training. Hopefully, all TAs have the opportunity to participate is this kind of feedback, and in doing so have a chance to develop their skills.

All of the formats in Chapter 6 for planning and monitoring, including the In-Class Support Agenda, might be of use when discussing TA performance and identifying ongoing training needs. It can also be a useful checklist against which to address concerns if conversations about performance and expectations are unstructured or overdue.

There are a number of SEND specific training opportunities for TAs wishing to learn more about this field. Introduced in 2003, the HLTA standards have formed the framework for the qualification of over 50,000 TAs as HLTAs. While the non-statutory draft standards for TAs and the HLTA share the same core and themes, HLTAs are expected to be able to demonstrate the ability to lead whole class teaching independently.

It's also possible to undertake accredited qualifications and training courses in supporting the learning of pupils with SpLDS, run by charitable organisations like Dyslexia Action, the Autistic Society and the Helen Arkell Centre. There are also numerous commercial providers of online courses about SEND for TAs at all levels.

Summary

The importance of shared practice

- This section explores the notion of sharing as a key aspect of the TA role.
- Working collaboratively can be supported by using the planning tools in Chapter 6.
- Addressing setbacks and criticism requires a thoughtful approach – see the list on page 146.
- It's important to get into good habits for sharing with colleagues – see the list on page 147.
- Education is a dynamic and ever-changing field; access to appropriate CPD is, therefore, essential to the entire school workforce.
- Working with one or more colleagues to support ongoing CPD cannot only address gaps in knowledge and skills, but build self-esteem, provide mutual support and help find solutions more quickly.
- It may be possible to extend knowledge and skills by undertaking professional courses, including the HLTA qualification or specialist training courses provided by the charitable and commercial sectors.

Bibliography

Chapter 1

Assets.publishing.service.gov.uk. 2020a. *Special Educational Needs and Disability Code of Practice: 0 to 25 Years*. [online] Available at: <https://assets.publishing.service.gov.uk/government/uploads/system/uploads/attachment_data/file/398815/SEND_Code_of_Practice_January_2015.pdf> [Accessed 16 April 2020].

Assets.publishing.service.gov.uk. 2020b. *Special Educational Needs in England: January 2019*. [online] Available at: <https://assets.publishing.service.gov.uk/government/uploads/system/uploads/attachment_data/file/814244/SEN_2019_Text.docx.pdf> [Accessed 16 April 2020].

Assets.publishing.service.gov.uk. 2020c. *Statements of SEN and EHC Plans: England, 2019*. [online] Available at: <https://assets.publishing.service.gov.uk/government/uploads/system/uploads/attachment_data/file/805014/SEN2_2019_text.pdf> [Accessed 16 April 2020].

Explore-education-statistics.service.gov.uk. 2020. *Education, Health and Care Plans, Reporting Year 2020*. [online] Available at: <https://explore-education-statistics.service.gov.uk/find-statistics/education-health-and-care-plans> [Accessed 11 May 2020].

Florian, L., 1998. Inclusive Practice: What? Why? and How? In: C. Tilstone, L. Florian & R. Rose (eds.) *Promoting Inclusive Practice*. London: Routledge.

Legislation.gov.uk. 2020a. *Children and Families Act 2014*. [online] Available at: <www.legislation.gov.uk/ukpga/2014/6/contents/enacted> [Accessed 16 April 2020].

Legislation.gov.uk. 2020b. *Education Act 1918*. [online] Available at: <www.legislation.gov.uk/ukpga/Geo5/8-9/39/enacted?view=plain> [Accessed 16 April 2020].

Legislation.gov.uk. 2020c. *Education Act 1981*. [online] Available at: <www.legislation.gov.uk/ukpga/1981/60/enacted> [Accessed 16 April 2020].

Legislation.gov.uk. 2020d. *Education Act 1993*. [online] Available at: <www.legislation.gov.uk/ukpga/1993/35/contents/enacted> [Accessed 16 April 2020].

Legislation.gov.uk. 2020e. *Education Act 1996*. [online] Available at: <www.legislation.gov.uk/ukpga/1996/56/contents> [Accessed 16 April 2020].

Legislation.gov.uk. 2020f. *Equality Act 2010*. [online] Available at: <www.legislation.gov.uk/ukpga/2010/15/contents> [Accessed 16 April 2020].

Legislation.gov.uk. 2020g. *The Special Educational Needs and Disability Regulations 2014*. [online] Available at: <www.legislation.gov.uk/uksi/2014/1530/contents/made> [Accessed 16 April 2020].

Ofsted. 2000. *Evaluating Educational Inclusion: Guidance for Inspectors and Schools*. London: Office for Standards in Education.

Publications.parliament.uk. 2020. *Special Educational Needs and Disabilities*. [online] Available at: <https://publications.parliament.uk/pa/cm201919/cmselect/cmeduc/20/20.pdf> [Accessed 16 April 2020].

The United Nations. 2006. *Convention on the Rights of Persons with Disabilities*. Treaty Series, 2515, 3.

Warnock Committee. 1978. *Special Educational Needs: The Warnock Report*. London: Department of Education and Science.

Chapter 2

Assets.publishing.service.gov.uk. 2020a. *School Workforce in England: November 2018*. [online] Available at: <https://assets.publishing.service.gov.uk/government/uploads/system/uploads/attachment_data/file/811622/SWFC_MainText.pdf> [Accessed 16 April 2020].

Assets.publishing.service.gov.uk. 2020b. *Special Educational Needs in England: January 2019*. [online] Available at: <https://assets.publishing.service.gov.uk/government/uploads/system/uploads/attachment_data/file/814244/SEN_2019_Text.docx.pdf> [Accessed 16 April 2020].

GOV.UK. 2011. *Teachers' Standards*. [online] Available at: <www.gov.uk/government/publications/teachers-standards> [Accessed 5 May 2020].

GOV.UK. 2015. *SEND Code of Practice: 0 to 25 Years*. [online] Available at: <www.gov.uk/government/publications/send-code-of-practice-0-to-25> [Accessed 5 May 2020].

GOV.UK. 2019. *Education Inspection Framework (EIF)*. [online] Available at: <www.gov.uk/government/publications/education-inspection-framework> [Accessed 5 May 2020].

Legislation.gov.uk. 2012. *The Education (Specified Work) (England) Regulations 2012*. [online] Available at: <www.legislation.gov.uk/uksi/2012/762/contents/made> [Accessed 9 May 2020].

Maximisingtas.co.uk. 2020. *Deployment and Impact of Support Staff in Schools*. [online] Available at: <http://maximisingtas.co.uk/assets/content/disss1w123r.pdf> [Accessed 16 April 2020].

Sharples, J., Webster, R. & Blatchford, P., 2020. *Making Best Use of Teaching Assistants*. [online] Discovery.ucl.ac.uk. Available at: <https://discovery.ucl.ac.uk/id/eprint/10068445/1/Sharples_TA_Guidance_Report_MakingBestUseOfTeachingAssistants-Printable.pdf> [Accessed 16 April 2020].

Bestpractice. 2020. www.bestpracticenet.co.uk/sites/default/files/resource-downloads/HLTA%20status%20and%20HLTA%20standards%20-%20what%20schools%20need%20to%20know.pdf.

The Code. (2005). https://assets.publishing.service.gov.uk/government/uploads/system/uploads/attachment_data/file/398815/SEND_Code_of_Practice_January_2015.pdf

Chapter 3

Assets.publishing.service.gov.uk. 2020. *Special Educational Needs in England: January 2019*. [online] Available at: <https://assets.publishing.service.gov.uk/

government/uploads/system/uploads/attachment_data/file/814244/SEN_2019_Text.docx.pdf> [Accessed 16 April 2020].

Oed.com. 2020. *Home: Oxford English Dictionary*. [online] Available at: <www.oed.com/> [Accessed 23 April 2020].

Pearsonassessments.com. 2020. *Pearson Assessments*. [online] Available at: <www.pearsonassessments.com> [Accessed 23 April 2020].

Wagner, R. K. & Torgesen, J. K., 1987. The nature of phonological processing and its causal role in the acquisition of reading skills. *Psychological Bulletin*, *101*(2), 192–212.

Chapter 5

Alexander-Passe, N., 2015. *Dyslexia and Mental Health*. London: Jessica Kingsley.

Alloway, R. & Alloway, T., 2013. *The Working Memory Advantage*. New York: Simon and Schuster.

Assets.publishing.service.gov.uk. 2019. [online] Available at: <https://assets.publishing.service.gov.uk/government/uploads/system/uploads/attachment_data/file/807862/Timpson_review.pdf> [Accessed 6 May 2020].

Assets.publishing.service.gov.uk. 2020. *Special Educational Needs and Disability Code of Practice: 0 to 25 Years*. [online] Available at: <https://assets.publishing.service.gov.uk/government/uploads/system/uploads/attachment_data/file/398815/SEND_Code_of_Practice_January_2015.pdf> [Accessed 16 April 2020].

Bartlett, J., 2016. *Outstanding Differentiation for Classroom Learning*. First ed. London and New York: David Fulton/Routledge.

Dweck, C., 2017. *Mindset*. London, UK: Little, Brown Book Company.

Education Endowment Foundation, 2020. *Standardised Tests | Assessing and Monitoring Pupil Progress*. [online] Available at: <https://educationendowmentfoundation.org.uk/tools/assessing-and-monitoring-pupil-progress/testing/standardised-tests/> [Accessed 12 May 2020].

Eide, B.L. & Eide, F.F., 2011. *The Dyslexia Advantage*. London and New York: Hay House.

EFF. 2005. https://educationendowmentfoundation.org.uk/public/files/Publications/Teaching_Assistants/TA_Guidance_Report_MakingBestUseOfTeachingAssistants-Printable.pdf

Elliot, V. et al., 2016. *A Marked Improvement? A Review of the Evidence of Written Marking*. London: EEF/University of Oxford.

GOV.UK. 2020. *Education Inspection Framework (EIF)*. [online] Available at: <www.gov.uk/government/publications/education-inspection-framework> [Accessed 23 April 2020].

Gray, A., 2018. *Effective Differentiation*. London: Routledge.

NHS Digital. 2018. *Measures From The Adult Social Care Outcomes Framework, England – 2017–18 – NHS Digital*. [online] Available at: <https://digital.nhs.uk/data-and-information/publications/statistical/adult-social-care-outcomes-framework-ascof/current> [Accessed 12 May 2020].

Sharples, J., Webster, R. & Blatchford, P., 2015. *Making Best Use of Teaching Assistants Guidance Report*. London: Education Endowment Foundation.

Workload Review Group. 2016. Eliminating unnecessary workload around marking' Report of the Independent Teacher Workload Review Group. Crown Publishers 2016

Chapter 6

Assets.publishing.service.gov.uk. 2020. *Special Educational Needs and Disability Code of Practice: 0 to 25 Years.* [online] Available at: <https://assets.publishing.service.gov.uk/government/uploads/system/uploads/attachment_data/file/398815/SEND_Code_of_Practice_January_2015.pdf> [Accessed 16 April 2020].

Education Endowment Foundation. 2020. *Teaching and Learning Toolkit.* [online] Available at: <https://educationendowmentfoundation.org.uk/evidence-summaries/teaching-learning-toolkit/#closeSignup> [Accessed 7 May 2020].

GOV.UK. 2019. *Education Inspection Framework (EIF).* [online] Available at: <www.gov.uk/government/publications/education-inspection-framework> [Accessed 6 May 2020].

Chapter 7

DFE & DoH, 2015. https://assets.publishing.service.gov.uk/government/uploads/system/uploads/attachment_data/file/398815/SEND_Code_of_Practice_January_2015.pdf

Honeybourne, V. 2018. *The Neurodiverse Classroom: A Teacher's Guide to Individual Learning Needs and How to Meet Them.* Jessica Kingsley Publishers, London and Philadelphia

Index

Note: Page numbers in *italics* indicate a figure and page numbers in **bold** indicate a table on the corresponding page.